Harvard
Business
Review

ON
EFFECTIVE
COMMUNICATION

THE HARVARD BUSINESS REVIEW PAPERBACK SERIES

The series is designed to bring today's managers and professionals the fundamental information they need to stay competitive in a fast-moving world. From the preeminent thinkers whose work has defined an entire field to the rising stars who will redefine the way we think about business, here are the leading minds and landmark ideas that have established the *Harvard Business Review* as required reading for ambitious businesspeople in organizations around the globe.

Other books in the series:

Harvard
Business
Review

ON
EFFECTIVE
COMMUNICATION

A HARVARD BUSINESS REVIEW PAPERBACK

The *Harvard Business Review* articles in this collection are available as individual reprints. Discounts apply to quantity purchases. For information and ordering, please contact Customer Service, Harvard Business School Publishing, Boston, MA 02163. Telephone: (617) 783-7500 or (800) 988-0886, 8 A.M. to 6 P.M. Eastern Time, Monday through Friday. Fax: (617) 783-7555, 24 hours a day. E-mail: custserv@hbsp.harvard.edu.

978-1-57851-143-3 (ISBN 13)
Library of Congress Cataloging-in-Publication Data
Harvard business review on effective communication.
        p.   cm. — (A Harvard business review paperback)
    Contains articles previously published in the Harvard business review.
    Includes index.
    ISBN 1-57851-143-7
    1. Business communication.   I. Harvard business review.
II. Series: Harvard business review paperback series.
HF5718.H292 1999
658.4'5—dc21   99-18897
                                                                        CIP

Contents

Harvard Business Review

ON

EFFECTIVE
COMMUNICATION

Listening to People

RALPH G. NICHOLS AND
LEONARD A. STEVENS

Executive Summary

"THE EFFECTIVENESS OF the spoken word," say Ralph
G. Nichols and Leonard A. Stevens, "hinges not so
much on how people talk but mostly on how they listen."
In their article, *Listening to People,* they open up a subject of tremendous practical importance to executives.
They go on to analyze the problem and discuss steps
for improving aural skills.

RECENTLY THE TOP EXECUTIVES of a major manufacturing plant in the Chicago area were asked to
survey the role that listening plays in their work. Later,
an executive seminar on listening was held. Here are
three typical comments made by participants:

- Frankly, I had never thought of listening as an important subject by itself. But now that I am aware of it, I think that perhaps 80% of my work depends on my listening to someone, or on someone else listening to me."

- "I've been thinking back about things that have gone wrong over the past couple of years, and I suddenly realized that many of the troubles have resulted from someone not hearing something, or getting it in a distorted way."

- "It's interesting to me that we have considered so many facets of communication in the company, but have inadvertently overlooked listening. I've about decided that it's the most important link in the company's communications, and it's obviously also the weakest one."

These comments reflect part of an awakening that is taking place in a number of management circles. Business is tied together by its systems of communication. This communication, businessmen are discovering, depends more on the spoken word than it does on the written word; and the effectiveness of the spoken word hinges not so much on how people talk as on how they listen.

The Unused Potential

It can be stated, with practically no qualification, that people in general do not know how to listen. They have ears that hear very well, but seldom have they acquired the necessary aural skills which would allow those ears to be used effectively for what is called *listening*.

For several years we have been testing the ability of people to understand and remember what they hear. At the University of Minnesota we examined the listening ability of several thousand students and of hundreds of business and professional people. In each case the person tested listened to short talks by faculty members and was examined for his grasp of the content.

These extensive tests led us to this general conclusion: immediately after the average person has listened to someone talk, he remembers only about half of what he has heard—no matter how carefully he thought he was listening.

What happens as time passes? Our own testing shows—and it has been substantiated by reports of research at Florida State University and Michigan State University[1]—that two months after listening to a talk, the average listener will remember only about 25% of what was said. In fact, after we have barely learned something, we tend to forget from one-half to one-third of it *within eight hours;* it is startling to realize that frequently we forget more in this first short interval than we do in the next six months.

Gap In Training

Behind this widespread inability to listen lies, in our opinion, a major oversight in our system of classroom instruction. We have focused attention on reading, considering it the primary medium by which we learn, and we have practically forgotten the art of listening. About six years are devoted to formal reading instruction in our school systems. Little emphasis is placed on speaking, and almost no attention has been given to the skill of listening, strange as this may be in view of the fact that so much lecturing is done in college. Listening training—if it could be called training—has often consisted merely of a series of admonitions extending from the first grade through college: "Pay attention!" "Now get this!" "Open your ears!" "Listen!"

Certainly our teachers feel the need for good listening. Why then have so many years passed without educators developing formal methods of teaching students to listen? We have been faced with several false assumptions which have blocked the teaching of listening. For example:

1. We have assumed that listening ability depends largely on intelligence, that "bright" people listen well, and "dull" ones poorly. There is no denying that low intelligence has something to do with inability to listen, but we have greatly exaggerated its importance. A poor listener is not necessarily an unintelligent person. To be good listeners we must apply certain skills that are acquired through either experience or training. If a person has not acquired these listening skills, his ability to understand and retain what he hears will be low. This can happen to people with both high and low levels of intelligence.

2. We have assumed that learning to read will automatically teach one to listen. While some of the skills attained through reading apply to listening, the assumption is far from completely valid. Listening is a different activity from reading and requires different skills. Research has shown that reading and listening skills do not improve at the same rate when only reading is taught.

This means that in our schools, where little attention is paid to the aural element of communication, reading ability is continually upgraded while listening ability, left to falter along on its own, actually degenerates. As a fair reader and a bad listener, the typical student is graduated into a society where the chances are high that he will have to listen about three times as much as he reads.

The barriers to listening training that have been built up by such false assumptions are coming down. Educators are realizing that listening is a skill that can be taught. In Nashville, for example, the public school system has started training in listening from elementary grades through high school. Listening is also taught in the Phoenix school system, in Cincinnati, and throughout the state of North Dakota. About two dozen major universities and colleges in the country now provide courses in listening.

At the University of Minnesota we have been presenting a course in listening to a large segment of the freshman class. Each group of students that has taken listening training has improved at least 25% in ability to understand the spoken word. Some of the groups have improved as much as 40%. We have also given a course in listening for adult education classes made up mostly of business and professional people. These people have made some of the highest gains in listening ability of any that we have seen. During one period, 60 men and women nearly doubled their listening test scores after working together on this skill one night a week for 17 weeks.

Ways to Improvement

Any course or any effort that will lead to listening improvement should do two things:

1. Build awareness to factors that affect listening ability.

2. Build the kind of aural experience that can produce good listening habits.

At least a start on the first of these two educational elements can be made by readers of this article; a certain degree of awareness is developed by merely discussing factors that affect listening ability. Later we shall discuss some steps that might be taken in order to work at the second element.

TRACKS AND SIDETRACKS

In general, people feel that concentration while listening is a greater problem than concentration during any other form of personal communication. Actually, listening concentration *is* more difficult. When we listen, concentration must be achieved despite a factor that is peculiar to aural communication, one of which few people are aware.

Basically, the problem is caused by the fact that we think much faster than we talk. The average rate of speech for most Americans is around 125 words per minute. This rate is slow going for the human brain, which is made up of more than 13 billion cells and operates in such a complicated but efficient manner that it makes the great, modern digital computers seem slow-witted. People who study the brain are not in complete agreement on how it functions when we think, but most psychologists believe that the basic medium of thought is language. Certainly words play a large part in our thinking processes, and the words race through our brains at speeds much higher than 125 words per minute. This means that, when we listen, we ask our brain to receive words at an extremely slow pace compared with its capabilities.

It might seem logical to slow down our thinking when we listen so as to coincide with the 125-word-per-minute speech rate, but slowing down thought processes seems to be a very difficult thing to do. When we listen, therefore, we continue thinking at high speed while the spoken words arrive at low speed. In the act of listening, the differential between thinking and speaking rates means that our brain works with hundreds of words in addition to those that we hear, assembling thoughts other than those spoken to us. To phrase it another way, we can listen and still have some spare time for thinking.

The use, or misuse, of this spare thinking time holds the answer to how well a person can concentrate on the spoken word.

Case of the disenchanted listener. In our studies at the University of Minnesota, we find most people do not use their spare thinking time wisely as they listen. Let us illustrate how this happens by describing a familiar experience:

> *A, the boss, is talking to B, the subordinate, about a new program that the firm is planning to launch. B is a poor listener. In this instance, he tries to listen well, but he has difficulty concentrating on what A has to say.*
>
> *A starts talking and B launches into the listening process, grasping every word and phrase that comes into his ears. But right away B finds that, because of A's slow rate of speech, he has time to think of things other than the spoken line of thought. Subconsciously, B decides to sandwich a few thoughts of his own into the aural ones that are arriving so slowly. So B quickly dashes out onto a*

mental sidetrack and thinks something like this: "Oh, yes, before I leave I want to tell A about the big success of the meeting I called yesterday." Then B comes back to A's spoken line of thought and listens for a few more words.

There is plenty of time for B to do just what he has done, dash away from what he hears and then return quickly, and he continues taking sidetracks to his own private thoughts. Indeed, he can hardly avoid doing this because over the years the process has become a strong aural habit of his.

But, sooner or later, on one of the mental sidetracks, B is almost sure to stay away too long. When he returns, A is moving along ahead of him. At this point it becomes harder for B to understand A, simply because B has missed part of the oral message. The private mental sidetracks become more inviting than ever, and B slides off onto several of them. Slowly he misses more and more of what A has to say.

When A is through talking, it is safe to say that B will have received and understood less than half of what was spoken to him.

Rules for Good Reception

A major task in helping people to listen better is teaching them to use their spare thinking time efficiently as they listen. What does "efficiently" mean? To answer this question, we made an extensive study of people's listening habits, especially trying to discover what happens when people listen well.

We found that good listeners regularly engage in four mental activities, each geared to the oral discourse and taking place concurrently with that oral discourse. All four of these mental activities are neatly coordinated when listening works at its best. They tend to direct a maximum amount of thought to the message being received, leaving a minimum amount of time for mental excursions on sidetracks leading away from the talker's thought. Here are the four processes:

1. The listener thinks ahead of the talker, trying to anticipate what the oral discourse is leading to and what conclusions will be drawn from the words spoken at the moment.

2. The listener weighs the evidence used by the talker to support the points that he makes. "Is this evidence valid?" the listener asks himself. "Is it the complete evidence?"

3. Periodically the listener reviews and mentally summarizes the points of the talk completed thus far.

4. Throughout the talk, the listener "listens between the lines" in search of meaning that is not necessarily put into spoken words. He pays attention to nonverbal communication (facial expressions, gestures, tone of voice) to see if it adds meaning to the spoken words. He asks himself, "Is the talker purposely skirting some area of the subject? Why is he doing so?"

The speed at which we think compared to that at which people talk allows plenty of time to accomplish these four mental tasks when we listen; however, they do require practice before they can become part of the mental agility that makes for good listening. In our training courses we have devised aural exercises designed to give people this practice and thereby build up good habits of aural concentration.

LISTENING FOR IDEAS

Another factor that affects listening ability concerns the reconstruction of orally communicated thoughts once they have been received by the listener. To illustrate:

> *The newspapers reported not too long ago that a church was torn down in Europe and shipped stone by stone to America, where it was reassembled in its original form. The moving of the church is analogous to what happens when a person speaks and is understood by a listener. The talker has a thought. To transmit his thought, he takes it apart by putting it into words. The words, sent through the air to the listener, must then be mentally reassembled into the original thought if they are to be thoroughly understood. But most people do not know what to listen for, and so cannot reconstruct the thought.*

For some reason many people take great pride in being able to say that above all they try to "get the facts" when they listen. It seems logical enough to do so. If a person gets all the facts, he should certainly understand what is said to him. Therefore, many people try to memorize every single fact that is spoken. With such practice at "getting the facts," the listener, we can safely assume, will develop a serious bad listening habit.

Memorizing facts is, to begin with, a virtual impossibility for most people in the listening situation. As one fact is being memorized, the whole, or part, of the next fact is almost certain to be missed. When he is doing his very best, the listener is likely to catch only a few facts, garble many others, and completely miss the remainder. Even in the case of people who *can* aurally assimilate all the facts that they hear, one at a time as they hear them, listening is still likely to be at a low level; they are concerned with the pieces of what they hear and tend to miss the broad areas of the spoken communication.

When people talk, they want listeners to understand their *ideas.* The facts are useful chiefly for constructing the ideas. Grasping ideas, we have found, is the skill on which the good listener concentrates. He remembers facts only long enough to understand the ideas that are built from them. But then, almost miraculously, grasping an idea will help the listener to remember the supporting facts more effectively than does the person who goes after facts alone. This listening skill is one which definitely can be taught, one in which people can build experience leading toward improved aural communication.

EMOTIONAL FILTERS

In different degrees and in many different ways, listening ability is affected by our emotions.[2] Figuratively we reach up and mentally turn off what we do not want to hear. Or, on the other hand, when someone says what we especially want to hear, we open our ears wide, accepting everything—truths, half-truths, or fiction. We might say, then, that our emotions act as aural filters. At times they in effect cause deafness, and at other times they make listening altogether too easy.

If we hear something that opposes our most deeply rooted prejudices, notions, convictions, mores, or complexes, our brains may become overstimulated, and not in a direction that leads to good listening. We mentally plan a rebuttal to what we hear, formulate a question designed to embarrass the talker, or perhaps simply turn to thoughts that support our own feelings on the subject at hand. For example:

*The firm's accountant goes to the general manager and
says: "I have just heard from the Bureau of Internal Revenue, and. . . ." The general manager suddenly
breathes harder as he thinks, "That blasted bureau!
Can't they leave me alone? Every year the government
milks my profits to a point where. . . ." Red in the face,
he whirls and stares out the window. The label "Bureau
of Internal Revenue" cuts loose emotions that stop the
general manager's listening.*

*In the meantime, the accountant may go on to say
that here is a chance to save $3,000 this year if the gen-
eral manager will take a few simple steps. The fuming
general manager may hear this—if the accountant
presses hard enough—but the chances are he will fail to
comprehend it.*

When emotions make listening too easy, it usually
results from hearing something which supports the
deeply rooted inner feelings that we hold. When we hear
such support, our mental barriers are dropped and
everything is welcomed. We ask few questions about
what we hear; our critical faculties are put out of commission by our emotions. Thinking drops to a minimum
because we are hearing thoughts that we have harbored
for years in support of our inner feelings. It is good to
hear someone else think those thoughts, so we lazily
enjoy the whole experience.

What can we do about these emotional filters? The
solution is not easy in practice, although it can be
summed up in this simple admonition: *hear the man out.*
Following are two pointers that often help in training
people to do this:

1. **Withhold evaluation**—This is one of the most
   important principles of learning, especially learning

through the ear. It requires self-control, sometimes more than many of us can muster, but with persistent practice it can be turned into a valuable habit. While listening, the main object is to comprehend each point made by the talker. Judgments and decisions should be reserved until after the talker has finished. At that time, and only then, review his main ideas and assess them.

2. **Hunt for negative evidence**—When we listen, it is human to go on a militant search for evidence which proves us right in what we believe. Seldom do we make a search for evidence to prove ourselves wrong. The latter type of effort is not easy, for behind its application must lie a generous spirit and real breadth of outlook. However, an important part of listening comprehension is found in the search for negative evidence in what we hear. If we make up our minds to seek out the ideas that might prove us wrong, as well as those that might prove us right, we are less in danger of missing what people have to say.

Benefits in Business

The improvement of listening, or simply an effort to make people aware of how important their listening ability is, can be of great value in today's business. When people in business fail to hear and understand each other, the results can be costly. Such things as numbers, dates, places, and names are especially easy to confuse, but the most straightforward agreements are often subjects of listening errors, too. When these mistakes are compounded, the resulting cost and inefficiency in business communication become serious. Building awareness of the importance of listening among employees can eliminate a large percentage of this type of aural error.

What are some of the specific problems which better listening can help solve?

LESS PAPER WORK

For one thing, it leads to economy of communication. Incidents created by poor listening frequently give businessmen a real fear of oral communication. As a result, they insist that more and more communication should be put into writing. A great deal of communication needs to be on the record, but the pressure to write is often carried too far. The smallest detail becomes "memoed." Paper work piles higher and higher and causes part of the tangle we call red tape. Many times less writing and more speaking would be advisable—*if* we could plan on good listening.

Writing and reading are much slower communication elements than speaking and listening. They require more personnel, more equipment, and more space than do speaking and listening. Often a stenographer and a messenger are needed, to say nothing of dictating machines, typewriters, and other writing materials. Few people ever feel it is safe to throw away a written communication; so filing equipment is needed, along with someone to do the filing.

In oral communication there are more human senses at work than in the visual; and if there is good listening, more can often be communicated in one message. And, perhaps most important of all, there is the give-and-take feature of oral communication. If the listener does not understand a message, he has the opportunity to straighten matters out then and there.

UPWARD COMMUNICATION

The skill of listening becomes extremely important when we talk about "upward communication." There are many avenues through which management can send messages downward through a business organization, but there are few avenues for movement of information in the upward direction. Perhaps the most obvious of the upward avenues is the human chain of people talking to people: the man working at the bench talks to his foreman, the foreman to his superintendent, the superintendent to his boss; and, relayed from person to person, the information eventually reaches the top.

This communication chain has potential, but it seldom works well because it is full of bad listeners. There can be failure for at least three reasons:

- Without good listeners, people do not talk freely and the flow of communication is seldom set in motion.

- If the flow should start, only one bad listener is needed to stop its movement toward the top.

- Even if the flow should continue to the top, the messages are likely to be badly distorted along the way.

It would be absurd to assume that these upward communication lines could be made to operate without hitches, but there is no reason to think that they cannot be improved by better listening. But the first steps must be taken by top management people. More and better listening on their part can prime the pumps that start the upward flow of information.

HUMAN RELATIONS

People in all phases of business need to feel free to talk to their superiors and to know they will be met with sympathetic understanding. But too many superiors— although they announce that their doors are always open—fail to listen; and their subordinates, in the face of this failure, do not feel free to say what they want to say. As a result, subordinates withdraw from their superiors more and more. They fail to talk about important problems that should be aired for both parties' benefit. When such problems remain unaired, they often turn into unrealistic monsters that come back to plague the superior who failed to listen.

The remedy for this sort of aural failure—and it should be applied when subordinates feel the need to talk—is what we have called "nondirective listening." The listener hears, really tries to understand, and later shows understanding by taking action if it is required. Above all, during an oral discourse, the listener refrains from firing his own thoughts back at the person talking or from indicating his displeasure or disapproval by his mannerisms or gestures; he speaks up only to ask for clarification of a point.

Since the listener stands the chance of hearing that his most dearly held notions and ideas may be wrong, this is not an easy thing to do. To listen nondirectively without fighting back requires more courage than most of us can muster. But when nondirective listening can be applied, the results are usually worth the effort. The persons talking have a chance to unburden themselves. Equally important, the odds are better that the listener can counsel or act effectively when the time comes to make a move.

Listening is only one phase of human relations, only one aspect of the administrator's job; by itself it will solve no major problems. Yet the past experience of many executives and organizations leaves no doubt, in our opinion, that better listening can lead to a reduction of the human frictions which beset many businesses today.

LISTENING TO SELL

High-pressure salesmanship is rapidly giving way to low-pressure methods in the marketing of industrial and consumer goods. Today's successful salesman is likely to center his attention on the customer-problem approach of selling.

To put this approach to work, the skill of listening becomes an essential tool for the salesman, while his vocal agility becomes less important. *How* a salesman talks turns out to be relatively unimportant because *what* he says, when it is guided by his listening, gives power to the spoken word. In other words, the salesman's listening becomes an on-the-spot form of customer research that can immediately be put to work in formulating any sales talk.

Regardless of the values that listening may hold for people who live by selling, a great many sales organizations seem to hold to the conviction that glibness has magic. Their efforts at improvement are aimed mainly at the talking side of salesmanship. It is our conviction, however, that with the typical salesman the ability to talk will almost take care of itself, but the ability to listen is something in real need of improvement.

IN CONFERENCE

The most important affairs in business are conducted around conference tables. A great deal has been said and written about how to talk at a conference, how to compromise, how to get problem-centered, and how to cope with certain types of individuals. All these things can be very important, but too frequently the experts forget to say, "First and foremost you must learn to listen at a conference."

The reason for this is simple when we think of the basic purpose for holding almost any conference. People get together to contribute their different viewpoints, knowledge, and experience to members of the group, which then seeks the best of all the conferees' thinking to solve a common problem. If there is far more talking than listening at a conference, however, the oral contributions made to the group are hardly worth the breath required to produce them.

More and better listening at any conference is certain to facilitate the exchange of ideas so important to the success of a meeting. It also offers many other advantages; for example, when participants do a good job of listening, their conference is more likely to remain centered on the problem at hand and less likely to go off on irrelevant tangents.

The first steps toward improved conference listening can be taken by the group leader. If he will simply make an opening statement calling attention to the importance of listening, he is very likely to increase the participants' aural response. And if the leader himself does a good job of listening, he stands the chance of being imitated by the others in his group.

Conclusion

Some businessmen may want to take steps to develop a listening improvement program in their companies. Here are 14 suggestions designed to carry on what we hope this article has already started to do—build awareness of listening.

1. Devote an executive seminar, or seminars, to a discussion of the roles and functions of listening as a business tool.

2. Use the filmed cases now becoming available for management training programs.[3] Since these cases present the problem as it would appear in reality, viewers are forced to practice good listening habits in order to be sure of what is going on—and this includes not only hearing the sound track but also watching the facial mannerisms, gestures, and motions of the actors.

3. If possible, bring in qualified speakers and ask them to discuss listening with special reference to how it might apply to business. Such speakers are available at a number of universities where listening is being taught as a part of communication training.

4. Conduct a self-inventory by the employees regarding their listening on the job. Provide everyone with a simple form divided into spaces for each hour of the day. Each space should be further divided to allow the user to keep track of the amount of time spent in

reading, writing, speaking, and listening. Discuss the results of these forms after the communication times have been totaled. What percentage of the time do people spend listening? What might improved listening mean in terms of job effectiveness?

5. Give a test in listening ability to people and show them the scores that they make. There is at least one standardized test for this purpose.[4] Discuss the meaning of the scores with the individuals tested.

6. Build up a library of spoken-word records of literature, speeches, and so forth (many can be purchased through record stores), and make them available in a room that has a record player. Also, lend the records to employees who might wish to take them home to enjoy them at their leisure. For such a library, material pertinent to the employees' jobs might be recorded so that those who are interested can listen for educational purposes.

7. Record a number of actual briefing sessions that may be held by plant superintendents or others. When new people go to work for the company, ask them to listen to these sessions as part of their initial training. Check their comprehension of what they hear by means of brief objective tests. Emphasize that this is being done because listening is important on the new jobs.

8. Set up role-playing situations wherein executives are asked to cope with complaints comparable to those that they might hear from subordinates. Ask observers to comment on how well an executive seems to listen. Do his remarks reflect a good job of listening? Does he keep himself from becoming

emotionally involved in what the subordinate says? Does the executive listen in a way which would encourage the subordinate to talk freely?

9. Ask salesmen to divide a notebook into sections, one for each customer. After making a call, a salesman should write down all useful information received aurally from the customer. As the information grows, he should refer to it before each return visit to a customer.

10. Where a sales organization has a number of friendly customers, invite some of the more articulate ones to join salesmen in a group discussion of sales techniques. How do the customers feel about talking and listening on the part of salesmen? Try to get the customers to make listening critiques of salesmen they encounter.

11. In a training session, plan and hold a conference on a selected problem and tape-record it. Afterwards, play back the recording. Discuss it in terms of listening. Do the oral contributions of different participants reflect good listening? If the conference should go off the track, try to analyze the causes in terms of listening.

12. If there is time after a regularly scheduled conference, hold a listening critique. Ask each member to evaluate the listening attention that he received while talking and to report his analysis of his own listening performance.

13. In important management meetings on controversial issues try Irving J. Lee's "Procedure for 'Coercing' Agreement."[5] Under the ground rules for this procedure, which Lee outlined in detail in his article,

the chairman calls for a period during which proponents of a hotly debated view can state their position without interruption; the opposition is limited to (a) the asking of questions for clarification, (b) requests for information concerning the peculiar characteristics of the proposal being considered;
and (c) requests for information as to whether it is possible to check the speaker's assumptions or predictions.

14. Sponsor a series of lectures for employees, their families, and their friends. The lectures might be on any number of interesting topics that have educational value as well as entertainment features. Point out that these lectures are available as part of a listening improvement program.

N OT ALL OF THESE SUGGESTIONS are applicable to every situation, of course. Each firm will have to adapt them to its own particular needs. The most important thing, however, may not be what happens when a specific suggestion is followed, but rather simply what happens when people become aware of the problem of listening and of what improved aural skills can do for their jobs and their businesses.

People seem to be far more powerfully driven to talk at each other than to listen to each other, and when they do listen the kind of feedback they give the speaker— and the kind of reaction the speaker makes, in turn, to this feedback—appears distressingly often to be self-defensive and generally competitive, or insincere and thus misleading, rather than clarifying, honest, and co-operative.

To be highlighted in this connection is the strangely underestimated fact that listeners can and frequently do feel gravely threatened by speakers. . . .

What makes this problem so intriguing is that as a matter of objective fact nothing passes from speaker to listener except air waves and light waves and, as such, as manifestations of physical force, they are impressively weak! Viewed mechanically, the sheer physical effects they sometimes produce are not obviously credible. These really feeble waves commonly disturb the cardio-vascular system, endocrine glands, autonomic nervous system, skeletal musculature, even the digestive system of the listener, with effects ranging all the way from increased heart rate and blanching of the skin to regurgitation and even loss of consciousness . . . . Meanwhile nothing except the gentlest of vibrations in the air and perfectly harmless reflections of light passes between speaker and listener—even when the speaker shouts, trembles, and jumps up and down violently. An effective awareness of this should go far to make listeners less fearful and speakers less confident of the threatening powers of words, particularly snarled or shouted words, as such.[6]

Notes

1. See E. J. J. Kramar and Thomas B. Lewis, "Comparison of Visual and Nonvisual Listening," *Journal of Communication*, November 1951, p. 16; and Arthur W. Heilman, "An Investigation in Measuring and Improving Listening Ability of College Freshmen," *Speech Monographs*, November 1951, p. 308.

2. See Wendell Johnson, "The Fateful Process of Mr. A Talking to Mr. B," *Harvard Business Review* January–February 1953, p. 49.

3. See George W. Gibson, "The Filmed Case in Management Training," *Harvard Business Review* May–June 1957, p. 123.

4. Brown-Carlsen Listening Comprehension Test (Yonkers-on-Hudson, World Book Company).

5. *Harvard Business Review* January–February 1954, p. 39.

6. Wendell Johnson, *Your Most Enchanted Listener,* New York, Harper & Brothers, 1956, pp. 184–186.

Originally published in September–October 1957
Reprint 57507

The material for this article comes from the authors' book, Are You Listening? *(New York, McGraw-Hill Book Company, Inc., scheduled for publication September, 1957).*

How to Run a Meeting

ANTONY JAY

Executive Summary

WHY IS IT THAT ANY SINGLE meeting may
be a waste of time, an irritant, or a barrier to the
achievement of an organization's objectives? The
answer lies in the fact, as the author says, that "all
sorts of human crosscurrents can sweep the discussion off course, and errors of psychology and technique on the chairman's part can defeat its purposes." This article offers guidelines on how to right
things that go wrong in meetings. The discussion
covers the functions of a meeting, the distinctions
in size and type of meetings, ways to define the objectives, making preparations, the chairman's role,
and ways to conduct a meeting that will achieve
its objectives.

Why have a meeting anyway? Why indeed? A great many important matters are quite satisfactorily conducted by a single individual who consults nobody. A great many more are resolved by a letter, a memo, a phone call, or a simple conversation between two people. Sometimes five minutes spent with six people separately is more effective and productive than a half-hour meeting with them all together.

Certainly a great many meetings waste a great deal of everyone's time and seem to be held for historical rather than practical reasons; many long-established committees are little more than memorials to dead problems. It would probably save no end of managerial time if every committee had to discuss its own dissolution once a year, and put up a case if it felt it should continue for another twelve months. If this requirement did nothing else, it would at least refocus the minds of the committee members on their purposes and objectives.

But having said that, and granting that "referring the matter to a committee" can be a device for diluting authority, diffusing responsibility, and delaying decisions, I cannot deny that meetings fulfill a deep human need. Man is a social species. In every organization and every human culture of which we have record, people come together in small groups at regular and frequent intervals, and in larger "tribal" gatherings from time to time. If there are no meetings in the places where they work, people's attachment to the organizations they work for will be small, and they will meet in regular formal or informal gatherings in associations, societies, teams, clubs, or pubs when work is over.

This need for meetings is clearly something more positive than just a legacy from our primitive hunting past. From time to time, some technomaniac or other comes up with a vision of the executive who never leaves his home, who controls his whole operation from an all-electronic, multichannel, microwave, fiber-optic video display dream console in his living room. But any manager who has ever had to make an organization work greets this vision with a smile that soon stretches into a yawn.

There is a world of science fiction, and a world of human reality; and those who live in the world of human reality know that it is held together by face-to-face meetings. A meeting still performs functions that will never be taken over by telephones, teleprinters, Xerox copiers, tape recorders, television monitors, or any other technological instruments of the information revolution.

Functions of a Meeting

At this point, it may help us understand the meaning of meetings if we look at the six main functions that meetings will always perform better than any of the more recent communication devices.

1. In the simplest and most basic way, a meeting defines the team, the group, or the unit. Those present belong to it; those absent do not. Everyone is able to look around and perceive the whole group and sense the collective identity of which he or she forms a part. We all know who we are—whether we are on the board of Universal International, in the overseas sales department of Flexitube, Inc., a member of the school management committee, on the East Hampton football team, or in Section No. 2 of Platoon 4, Company B.

2. A meeting is the place where the group revises, updates, and adds to what it knows *as a group*. Every group creates its own pool of shared knowledge, experience, judgment, and folklore. But the pool consists only of what the individuals have experienced or discussed as a group—i.e., those things which every individual knows that all the others know, too. This pool not only helps all members to do their jobs more intelligently, but it also greatly increases the speed and efficiency of all communications among them. The group knows that all special nuances and wider implications in a brief statement will be immediately clear to its members. An enormous amount of material can be left unsaid that would have to be made explicit to an outsider.

But this pool needs constant refreshing and replenishing, and occasionally the removal of impunities. So the simple business of exchanging information and ideas that members have acquired separately or in smaller groups since the last meeting is an important contribution to the strength of the group. By questioning and commenting on new contributions, the group performs an important "digestive" process that extracts what's valuable and discards the rest.

Some ethologists call this capacity to share knowledge and experience among a group "the social mind," conceiving it as a single mind dispersed among a number of skulls. They recognize that this "social mind" has a special creative power, too. A group of people meeting together can often produce better ideas, plans, and decisions than can a single individual, or a number of individuals, each working alone. The meeting can of course also produce worse outputs or none at all, if it is a bad meeting.

However, when the combined experience, knowledge, judgment, authority, and imagination of a half dozen people are brought to bear on issues, a great many plans and decisions are improved and sometimes transformed. The original idea that one person might have come up with singly is tested, amplified, refined, and shaped by argument and discussion (which often acts on people as some sort of chemical stimulant to better performance), until it satisfies far more requirements and overcomes many more objections than it could in its original form.

3. A meeting helps every individual understand both the collective aim of the group and the way in which his own and everyone else's work can contribute to the group's success.

4. A meeting creates in all present a commitment to the decisions it makes and the objectives it pursues. Once something has been decided, even if you originally argued against it, your membership in the group entails an obligation to accept the decision. The alternative is to leave the group, but in practice this is very rarely a dilemma of significance. Real opposition to decisions within organizations usually consists of one part disagreement with the decision to nine parts resentment at not being consulted before the decision. For most people on most issues, it is enough to know that their views were heard and considered. They may regret that they were not followed, but they accept the outcome.

And just as the decision of any team is binding on all the members, so the decisions of a meeting of people higher up in an organization carry a greater authority than any decision by a single executive. It is much harder to challenge a decision of the board than of the chief executive acting on his own. The decision-making authority of a meeting is of special importance for long-term policies and procedures.

5. In the world of management, a meeting is very often the only occasion where the team or group actually exists and works as a group, and the only time when the supervisor, manager, or executive is actually perceived as the leader of the team, rather than as the official to whom individuals report. In some jobs the leader does guide his team through his personal presence—not just the leader of a pit gang or construction team, but also the chef in the hotel kitchen and the maitre d'hôtel in the restaurant, or the supervisor in a department store. But in large administrative headquarters, the daily or weekly meeting is often the only time when the leader is ever perceived to be guiding a team rather than doing a job.

6. A meeting is a status arena. It is no good to pretend that people are not or should not be concerned with their status relative to the other members in a group. It is just another part of human nature that we have to live with. It is a not insignificant fact that the word *order* means (a) hierarchy or pecking order; (b) an instruction or command; and (c) stability and the way things ought to be, as in "put your affairs in order," or "law and order." All three definitions are aspects of the same idea, which is indivisible.

Since a meeting is so often the only time when members get the chance to find out their relative standing, the "arena" function is inevitable. When a group is new, has a new leader, or is composed of people like department heads who are in competition for promotion and who do not work in a single team outside the meeting, "arena behavior" is likely to figure more largely, even to the point of dominating the proceedings. However, it will hardly signify with a long-established group that meets regularly.

Despite the fact that a meeting can perform all of the foregoing main functions, there is no guarantee that it will do so in any given situation. It is all too possible that any single meeting may be a waste of time, an irritant, or a barrier to the achievement of the organization's objectives.

What Sort of Meeting?

While my purpose in this article is to show the critical points at which most meetings go wrong, and to indicate ways of putting them right, I must first draw some important distinctions in the size and type of meetings that we are dealing with.

Meetings can be graded by *size* into three broad categories: (1) the assembly—100 or more people who are expected to do little more than listen to the main speaker or speakers; (2) the council—40 or 50 people who are basically there to listen to the main speaker or speakers but who can come in with questions or comments and who may be asked to contribute something on their own account; and (3) the committee—up to 10 (or at the most 12) people, all of whom more or less speak on an equal footing under the guidance and control of a chairman.

We are concerned in this article only with the "committee" meeting though it may be described as a committee, a subcommittee, a study group, a project team, a working party, a board, or by any of dozens of other titles. It is by far the most common meeting all over the world, and can perhaps be traced back to the primitive hunting band through which our species evolved. Beyond doubt it constitutes the bulk of the 11 million meetings that—so it has been calculated—take place every day in the United States.

Apart from the distinction of size, there are certain considerations regarding the *type* of meeting that profoundly affect its nature. For instance:

Frequency—A daily meeting is different from a weekly one, and a weekly meeting from a monthly one. Irregular, ad hoc, quarterly, and annual meetings are different again. On the whole, the frequency of meetings defines—or perhaps even determines—the degree of unity of the group.

Composition—Do the members work together on the same project, such as the nursing and ancillary staff on the same ward of a hospital? Do they work on different but parallel tasks, like a meeting of the company's plant managers or regional sales managers? Or are they a diverse group—strangers to each other, perhaps—united only by the meeting itself and by a common interest in realizing its objectives?

Motivation—Do the members have a common objective in their work, like a football team? Or do they to some extent have a competitive working relationship, like managers of subsidiary companies at a meeting with the chief executive, or the heads of research, production, and marketing discussing finance allocation for the coming year? Or does the desire for success through the meeting itself unify them, like a neighborhood action group or a new product design committee?

Decision process—How does the meeting group ultimately reach its decisions? By a general consensus, "the feeling of the meeting"? By a majority vote? Or are the decisions left entirely to the chairman himself, after he has listened to the facts and opinions.

KINDS OF MEETINGS

The experienced meeting-goer will recognize that, although there seem to be five quite different methods of analyzing a meeting, in practice there is a tendency for certain kinds of meetings to sort themselves out into one of three categories. Consider:

The *daily meeting,* where people work together on the same project with a common objective and reach decisions informally by general agreement.

The *weekly* or *monthly meeting*, where members work on different but parallel projects and where there is a certain competitive element and a greater likelihood that the chairman will make the final decision himself.

The *irregular, occasional,* or *"special project" meeting*, composed of people whose normal work does not bring them into contact and whose work has little or no relationship to the others'. They are united only by the project the meeting exists to promote and motivated by the desire that the project should succeed.

Though actual voting is uncommon, every member effectively has a veto.

Of these three kinds of meetings, it is the first—the workface type—that is probably the most common. It is also, oddly enough, the one most likely to be successful. Operational imperatives usually ensure that it is brief, and the participants' experience of working side by side ensures that communication is good.

The other two types are a different matter. In these meetings all sorts of human crosscurrents can sweep the discussion off course, and errors of psychology and technique on the chairman's part can defeat its purposes. Moreover, these meetings are likely to bring together the more senior people and to produce decisions that profoundly affect the efficiency, prosperity, and even survival of the whole organization. It is, therefore, toward these higher-level meetings that the lessons of this article are primarily directed.

Before the Meeting

The most important question you should ask is: "What is this meeting intended to achieve?" You can ask it in different ways—"What would be the likely consequences of not holding it?" "When it is over, how shall I judge whether it was a success or a failure?"—but unless you have a very clear requirement from the meeting, there is a grave danger that it will be a waste of everyone's time.

DEFINING THE OBJECTIVE

You have already looked at the six main functions that all meetings perform, but if you are trying to use a meeting to achieve definite objectives, there are in practice only certain types of objectives it can really achieve. Every item on the agenda can be placed in one of the following four categories, or divided up into sections that fall into one or more of them.

1. **Informative-digestive**—Obviously, it is a waste of time for the meeting to give out purely factual information that would be better circulated in a document. But if the information should be heard from a particular person, or if it needs some clarification and comment to make sense of it, or if it has deep implications for the members of the meeting, then it is perfectly proper to introduce an item onto the agenda that requires no conclusion, decision, or action from the meeting, it is enough, simply, that the meeting should receive and discuss a report.

   The "informative-digestive" function includes progress reports—to keep the group up to date on the current status of projects it is responsible for or that affect its deliberations—and review of completed projects in order to come to a collective judgment and to see what can be learned from them for the next time.

2. **Constructive-originative**—This "What shall we do?" function embraces all items that require something new to be devised, such as a new policy, a new strategy, a new sales target, a new product, a new marketing plan, a new procedure, and so forth. This sort of discussion asks people to contribute their knowledge, experience, judgment, and ideas. Obviously, the plan will probably be inadequate unless all relevant parties are present and pitching in.

3. **Executive responsibilities**—This is the "How shall we do it?" function, which comes after it has been decided what the members are going to do; at this point, executive responsibilities for the different components of the task have to be distributed around the table. Whereas in the second function the contributors' importance is their knowledge and ideas, here their contribution is the responsibility for implementing the plan. The fact that they and their subordinates are affected by it makes their contribution especially significant.

It is of course possible to allocate these executive responsibilities without a meeting, by separate individual briefings, but several considerations often make a meeting desirable.

First, it enables the members as a group to find the best way of achieving the objectives.

Second, it enables each member to understand and influence the way in which his own job fits in with the jobs of the others and with the collective task.

Third, if the meeting is discussing the implementation of a decision taken at a higher level, securing the group's consent may be of prime importance. If so, the fact that the group has the opportunity to formulate the detailed action plan itself may be the decisive factor in securing its agreement, because in that case the final decision belongs, as it were, to the group. Everyone is committed to what the group decides and is collectively responsible for the final shape of the project, as well as individually answerable for his own part in it. Ideally, this sort of agenda item starts with a policy, and ends with an action plan.

4. **Legislative framework**—Above and around all considerations of "What to do" and "How to do it," there is a framework—a departmental or divisional organization—and a system of rules, routines, and procedures within and through which all the activity takes place. Changing this framework and introducing a new organization or new procedures can be deeply disturbing to committee members and a threat to their status and long-term security. Yet leaving it unchanged can stop the organization from adapting to a changing world. At whatever level this change happens, it must have the support of all the perceived leaders whose groups are affected by it.

The key leaders for this legislative function must collectively make or confirm the decision; if there is any important dissent, it is very dangerous to close the discussion and make the decision by decree. The group leaders cannot expect quick decisions if they are seeking to change the organization framework and routines that people have grown up with. Thus they must be prepared to leave these items unresolved for further discussion and consultation. As Francis Bacon put it—and it has never been put better—"Counsels to which time hath not been called, time will not ratify."

MAKING PREPARATIONS

The four different functions just discussed may of course be performed by a single meeting, as the group proceeds through the agenda. Consequently, it may be a useful exercise for the chairman to go through the agenda, writing beside each item which function it is intended to fulfill. This exercise helps clarify what is expected from the discussion and helps focus on which people to bring in and what questions to ask them.

People. The value and success of a committee meeting are seriously threatened if too many people are present. Between 4 and 7 is generally ideal, 10 is tolerable, and 12 is the outside limit. So the chairman should do everything he can to keep numbers down, consistent with the need to invite everyone with an important contribution to make.

The leader may have to leave out people who expect to come or who have always come. For this job he may need tact; but since people generally preserve a fiction that they are overworked already and dislike serving on committees, it is not usually hard to secure their consent to stay away.

If the leader sees no way of getting the meeting down to a manageable size, he can try the following devices: (a) analyze the agenda to see whether everyone has to be present for every item (he may be able to structure the agenda so that some people can leave at half time and others can arrive); (b) ask himself whether he doesn't really need two separate, smaller meetings rather than one big one; and (c) determine whether one or two groups can be asked to thrash some of the topics out in advance so that only one of them needs to come in with its proposals.

Remember, too, that a few words with a member on the day before a meeting can increase the value of the meeting itself, either by ensuring that an important point is raised that comes better from the floor than from the chair or by preventing a time-wasting discussion of a subject that need not be touched on at all.

Papers. The agenda is by far the most important piece
of paper. Properly drawn up, it has a power of speeding
and clarifying a meeting that very few people understand or harness. The main fault is to make it unneces-
sarily brief and vague. For example, the phrase "development budget" tells nobody very much, whereas the
longer explanation "To discuss the proposal for reduction of the 1976–1977 development budget now that the
introduction of our new product has been postponed"
helps all committee members to form some views or
even just to look up facts and figures in advance.

Thus the leader should not be afraid of a long agenda,
provided that the length is the result of his analyzing
and defining each item more closely, rather than of his
adding more items than the meeting can reasonably
consider in the time allowed. He should try to include,
very briefly, some indication of the reason for each topic
to be discussed. If one item is of special interest to the
group, it is often a good idea to single it out for special
mention in a covering note.

The leader should also bear in mind the useful device
of heading each item "For information," "For discussion," or "For decision" so that those at the meeting
know where they are trying to get to.

And finally, the chairman should not circulate the
agenda too far in advance, since the less organized
members will forget it or lose it. Two or three days is
about right—unless the supporting papers are volumi-
nous.

Other 'paper' considerations: The order of items on
the agenda is important. Some aspects are obvious—the
items that need urgent decision have to come before
those that can wait till next time. Equally, the leader
does not discuss the budget for the re-equipment pro-

gram before discussing whether to put the re-equipment off until next year. But some aspects are not so obvious. Consider:

- The early part of a meeting tends to be more lively and creative than the end of it, so if an item needs mental energy, bright ideas, and clear heads, it may be better to put it high up on the list. Equally, if there is one item of great interest and concern to everyone, it may be a good idea to hold it back for a while and get some other useful work done first. Then the star item can be introduced to carry the meeting over the attention lag that sets in after the first 15 to 20 minutes of the meeting.

- Some items unite the meeting in a common front while others divide the members one from another. The leader may want to start with unity before entering into division, or he may prefer the other way around. The point is to be aware of the choice and to make it consciously, because it is apt to make a difference to the whole atmosphere of the meeting. It is almost always a good idea to find a unifying item with which to end the meeting.

- A common fault is to dwell too long on trivial but urgent items, to the exclusion of subjects of fundamental importance whose significance is long-term rather than immediate. This can be remedied by putting on the agenda the time at which discussion of the important long-term issue will begin—and by sticking to it.

- Very few business meetings achieve anything of value after two hours, and an hour and a half is enough time to allocate for most purposes.

- It is often a good idea to put the finishing time of a meeting on the agenda as well as the starting time.

- If meetings have a tendency to go on too long, the chairman should arrange to start them one hour before lunch or one hour before the end of work. Generally, items that ought to be kept brief can be introduced ten minutes from a fixed end point.

- The practice of circulating background or proposal papers along with the minutes is, in principle, a good one. It not only saves time, but it also helps in formulating useful questions and considerations in advance. But the whole idea is sabotaged once the papers get too long; they should be brief or provide a short summary. If they are circulated, obviously the chairman has to read them, or at least must not be caught not having read them. (One chairman, more noted for his cunning than his conscientiousness, is said to have spent 30 seconds before each meeting going through all the papers he had not read with a thick red pen, marking lines and question marks in the margins at random, and making sure these were accidentally made visible to the meeting while the subject was being discussed.)

- If papers are produced at the meeting for discussion, they should obviously be brief and simple, since everyone has to read them. It is a supreme folly to bring a group of people together to read six pages of closely printed sheets to themselves. The exception is certain kinds of financial and statistical papers whose function is to support and illustrate verbal points as reference documents rather than to be swallowed whole: these are often better tabled at the meeting.

- All items should be thought of and thought about in advance if they are to be usefully discussed. Listing "Any other business" on the agenda is an invitation to waste time. This does not absolutely preclude the chairman's announcing an extra agenda item at a meeting if something really urgent and unforeseen crops up or is suggested to him by a member, provided it is fairly simple and straightforward. Nor does it preclude his leaving time for general unstructured discussion after the close of the meeting.

- The chairman, in going through the agenda items in advance, can usefully insert his own brief notes of points he wants to be sure are not omitted from the discussion. A brief marginal scribble of "How much notice?" or "Standby arrangements?" or whatever is all that is necessary.

The Chairman's Job

Let's say that you have just been appointed chairman of the committee. You tell everyone that it is a bore or a chore. You also tell them that you have been appointed "for my sins." But the point is that you tell them. There is no getting away from it: some sort of honor or glory attaches to the chairman's role. Almost everyone is in some way pleased and proud to be made chairman of something. And that is three quarters of the trouble.

MASTER OR SERVANT?

Their appointment as committee chairman takes people in different ways. Some seize the opportunity to impose their will on a group that they see themselves licensed to dominate. Their chairmanship is a harangue, interspersed with demands for group agreement.

Others are more like scoutmasters, for whom the collective activity of the group is satisfaction enough, with no need for achievement. Their chairmanship is more like the endless stoking and fueling or a campfire that is not cooking anything.

And there are the insecure or lazy chairmen who look to the meeting for reassurance and support in their ineffectiveness and inactivity, so that they can spread the responsibility for their indecisiveness among the whole group. They seize on every expression of disagreement or doubt as a justification for avoiding decision or action.

But even the large majority who do not go to those extremes still feel a certain pleasurable tumescence of the ego when they take their place at the head of the table for the first time. The feeling is no sin: the sin is to indulge it or to assume that the pleasure is shared by the other members of the meeting.

It is the chairman's self-indulgence that is the greatest single barrier to the success of a meeting. His first duty, then, is to be aware of the temptation and of the dangers of yielding to it. The clearest of the danger signals is hearing himself talking a lot during a discussion.

One of the best chairmen I have ever served under makes it a rule to restrict her interventions to a single sentence, or at most two. She forbids herself ever to contribute a paragraph to a meeting she is chairing. It is a harsh rule, but you would be hard put to find a regular attender of her meetings (or anyone else's) who thought it was a bad one.

There is, in fact, only one legitimate source of pleasure in chairmanship, and that is pleasure in the achievements of the meeting—and to be legitimate it must be shared by all those present. Meetings are *necessary* for all sorts of basic and primitive human reasons, but they are *useful* only if they are seen by all present to be getting somewhere—and somewhere they know they could not have gotten to individually.

If the chairman is to make sure that the meeting achieves valuable objectives, he will be more effective seeing himself as the servant of the group rather than as its master. His role then becomes that of assisting the group toward the best conclusion or decision in the most efficient manner possible: to interpret and clarify; to move the discussion forward; and to bring it to a resolution that everyone understands and accepts as being the will of the meeting, even if the individuals do not necessarily agree with it.

His true source of authority with the members is the strength of his perceived commitment to their combined objective and his skill and efficiency in helping and guiding them to its achievement. Control and discipline then become not the act of imposing his will on the group but of imposing the group's will on any individual who is in danger of diverting or delaying the progress of the discussion and so from realizing the objective.

Once the members realize that the leader is impelled by his commitment to their common objective, it does not take great force of personality for him to control the meeting. Indeed, a sense of urgency and a clear desire to reach the best conclusion as quickly as possible are a much more effective disciplinary instrument than a big gavel. The effective chairman can then hold the discussion to the point by indicating that there is no time to pursue a particular idea now, that there is no time for long speeches, that the group has to get through this item and on to the next one, rather than by resorting to pulling rank.

There are many polite ways the chairman can indicate a slight impatience even when someone else is speaking—by leaning forward, fixing his eyes on the speaker tensing his muscles, raising his eyebrows, or nodding briefly to show the point is taken. And when replying or commenting, the chairman can indicate by the speed, brevity, and finality of his intonation that "we have to move on." Conversely, he can reward the sort of contribution he is seeking by the opposite expressions and intonations, showing that there is plenty of time for that sort of idea, and encouraging the speaker to develop the point.

After a few meetings, all present readily understand this nonverbal language of chairmanship. It is the chairman's chief instrument of educating the group into the general type of "meeting behavior" that he is looking for. He is still the servant of the group, but like a hired mountain guide, he is the one who knows the destination, the route, the weather signs, and the time the journey will take. So if he suggests that the members walk a bit faster, they take his advice.

This role of servant rather than master is often obscured in large organizations by the fact that the chairman is frequently the line manager of the members: this does not, however, change the reality of the role of chairman. The point is easier to see in, say, a neighborhood action group. The question in that case is, simply, "Through which person's chairmanship do we collectively have the best chance of getting the children's playground built?"

However, one special problem is posed by this definition of the chairman's role, and it has an extremely interesting answer. The question is: How can the chairman combine his role with the role of a member advocating one side of an argument?

The answer comes from some interesting studies by researchers who sat in on hundreds of meetings to find out how they work. Their consensus finding is that most of the effective discussions have, in fact, two leaders: one they call a "team," or "social," leader; the other a "task," or "project," leader.

Regardless of whether leadership is in fact a single or a dual function, for our purposes it is enough to say that the chairman's best role is that of social leader. If he wants a particular point to be strongly advocated, he ensures that it is someone else who leads off the task discussion, and he holds back until much later in the argument. He might indeed change or modify his view through hearing the discussion, but even if he does not it is much easier for him to show support for someone else's point later in the discussion, after listening to the arguments. Then, he can summarize in favor of the one he prefers.

The task advocate might regularly be the chairman's second-in-command, or a different person might advocate for different items on the agenda. On some subjects, the chairman might well be the task advocate himself, especially if they do not involve conflict within the group. The important point is that the chairman has to keep his "social leadership" even if it means sacrificing his "task leadership." However, if the designated task advocate persists in championing a cause through two or three meetings, he risks building up quite a head of antagonism to him among the other members. Even so, this antagonism harms the group less by being directed at the "task leader" than at the "social leader."

STRUCTURE OF DISCUSSION

It may seem that there is no right way or wrong way to structure a committee meeting discussion.

A subject is raised, people say what they think, and finally a decision is reached, or the discussion is terminated. There is some truth in this. Moreover, it would be a mistake to try and tie every discussion of every item down to a single immutable format.

Nevertheless, there is a logical order to a group discussion, and while there can be reasons for not following it, there is no justification for not being aware of it. In practice, very few discussions are inhibited, and many are expedited, by a conscious adherence to the following stages, which follow exactly the same pattern as a visit to the doctor.

"What seems to be the trouble?" The reason for an item being on a meeting agenda is usually like the symptom we go to the doctor with: "I keep getting this pain in my back" is analogous to "Sales have risen in Germany but fallen in France." In both cases it is clear that something is wrong and that something ought to be done to put it right. But until the visit to the doctor, or the meeting of the European marketing committee, that is about all we really know.

"How long has this been going on?" The doctor will start with a case history of all the relevant background facts, and so will the committee discussion. A solid basis of shared and agreed-on facts is the best foundation to build any decision on, and a set of pertinent questions will help establish it. For example, when did French sales start to fall off? Have German sales risen exceptionally? Has France had delivery problems, or less sales effort, or weaker advertising? Have we lost market share, or are

our competitors' sales falling too? If the answers to all
these questions, and more, are not established at the
start, a lot of discussion may be wasted later.

"Would you just lie down on the couch?" The doctor
will then conduct a physical examination to find out
how the patient is now. The committee, too, will want to
know how things stand at this moment. Is action being
taken? Do long-term orders show the same trend? What
are the latest figures? What is the current stock position? How much money is left in the advertising budget?

"You seem to have slipped a disc." When the facts are
established, you can move toward a diagnosis. A doctor
may seem to do this quickly, but that is the result of
experience and practice. He is, in fact, rapidly eliminating all the impossible or far-fetched explanations until
he leaves himself with a short list. The committee, too,
will hazard and eliminate a variety of diagnoses until it
homes in on the most probable—for example the company's recent energetic and highly successful advertising
campaign in Germany plus new packaging by the market leader in France.

"Take this round to the druggist." Again, the doctor is
likely to take a shortcut that a committee meeting may
be wise to avoid. The doctor comes out with a single
prescription, and the committee, too, may agree quickly
on a single course of action.

But if the course is not so clear, it is better to take
this step in two stages: (a) construct a series of
options—do not, at first, reject any suggestions outright
but try to select and combine the promising elements
from all of them until a number of thought-out, coher-
ent, and sensible suggestions are on the table; and (b)
only when you have generated these options do you start
to choose among them. Then you can discuss and decide

whether to pick the course based on repackaging and point-of-sale promotion, or the one based on advertising and a price cut, or the one that bides its time and saves the money for heavier new-product promotion next year.

I<small>F THE ITEM IS AT ALL COMPLEX</small> or especially significant, it is important for the chairman not only to have the proposed course of the discussion in his own head, but also to announce it so that everyone knows. A good idea is to write the headings on an easel pad with a felt pen. This saves much of the time wasting and confusion that result when people raise items in the wrong place because they were not privy to the chairman's secret that the right place was coming up later on in the discussion.

Conducting the Meeting

Just as the driver of a car has two tasks, to follow his route and to manage his vehicle, so the chairman's job can be divided into two corresponding tasks, dealing with the subject and dealing with the people.

DEALING WITH THE SUBJECT

The essence of this task is to follow the structure of discussion as just described in the previous section. This, in turn, entails listening carefully and keeping the meeting pointed toward the objective.

At the start of the discussion of any item, the chairman should make it clear where the meeting should try to get to by the end. Are the members hoping to make a clear decision or firm recommendation? Is it a preliminary deliberation to give the members something to go away with and think about? Are they looking for a variety of different lines to be pursued outside the meeting? Do they have to approve the proposal, or merely note it?

The chairman may give them a choice: "If we can agree on a course of action, that's fine. If not, we'll have to set up a working party to report and recommend before next month's meeting."

The chairman should make sure that all the members understand the issue and why they are discussing it. Often it will be obvious, or else they may have been through it before. If not, then he or someone he has briefed before the meeting should give a short introduction, with some indication of the reason the item is on the agenda; the story so far; the present position; what needs to be established, resolved, or proposed; and some indication of lines of inquiry or courses of action that have been suggested or explored, as well as arguments on both sides of the issue.

If the discussion is at all likely to be long or complex, the chairman should propose to the meeting a structure for it with headings (written up if necessary), as I stated at the end of the section on "Structure of discussion." He should listen carefully in case people jump too far ahead (e.g., start proposing a course of action before the meeting has agreed on the cause of the trouble), or go back over old ground, or start repeating points that have been made earlier. He has to head discussion off sterile or irrelevant areas very quickly (e.g., the rights and wrongs of past decisions that it is too late to change, or distant prospects that are too remote to affect present actions).

It is the chairman's responsibility to prevent misunderstanding and confusion. If he does not follow an argument or understand a reference, he should seek clarification from the speaker. If he thinks two people are using the same word with different meanings, he should intervene (e.g., one member using *promotion* to mean point-of-sale advertising only, and another also including media publicity).

He may also have to clarify by asking people for facts or experience that perhaps influence their view but are not known to others in the meeting. And he should be on the lookout for points where an interim summary would be helpful. This device frequently takes only a few seconds, and acts like a life belt to some of the members who are getting out of their depth.

Sometimes a meeting will have to discuss a draft document. If there are faults in it, the members should agree on what the faults are and the chairman should delegate someone to produce a new draft later. The group should never try to redraft around the table.

Perhaps one of the most common faults of chairmanship is the failure to terminate the discussion early enough. Sometimes chairmen do not realize that the meeting has effectively reached an agreement, and consequently they let the discussion go on for another few minutes, getting nowhere at all. Even more often, they are not quick enough to close a discussion *before* agreement has been reached.

A discussion should be closed once it has become clear that (a) more facts are required before further progress can be made, (b) discussion has revealed that the meeting needs the views of people not present, (c) members need more time to think about the subject and perhaps discuss it with colleagues, (d) events are changing and likely to alter or clarify the basis of the decision quite soon, (e) there is not going to be enough time at this meeting to go over the subject properly, or (f) it is becoming clear that two or three of the members can settle this outside the meeting without taking up the time of the rest. The fact that the decision is difficult, likely to be disputed, or going to be unwelcome to somebody, however, is not a reason for postponement.

At the end of the discussion of each agenda item, the chairman should give a brief and clear summary of what has been agreed on. This can act as the dictation of the actual minutes. It serves not merely to put the item on record, but also to help people realize that something worthwhile has been achieved. It also answers the question "Where did all that get us?" If the summary involves action by a member of the meeting, he should be asked to confirm his acceptance of the undertaking.

DEALING WITH THE PEOPLE

There is only one way to ensure that a meeting starts on time, and that is to start it on time. Latecomers who find that the meeting has begun without them soon learn the lesson. The alternative is that the prompt and punctual members will soon realize that a meeting never starts until ten minutes after the advertised time, and they will also learn the lesson.

Punctuality at future meetings can be wonderfully reinforced by the practice of listing late arrivals (and early departures) in the minutes. Its ostensible and perfectly proper purpose is to call the latecomer's attention to the fact that he was absent when a decision was reached. Its side effect, however, is to tell everyone on the circulation list that he was late, and people do not want that sort of information about themselves published too frequently.

There is a growing volume of work on the significance of seating positions and their effect on group behavior and relationships. Not all the findings are generally agreed on. What does seem true is that:

- Having members sit face to face across a table facilitates opposition, conflict, and disagreement, though of course it does not turn allies into enemies. But it does suggest that the chairman should think about whom he seats opposite himself.

- Sitting side by side makes disagreements and confrontation harder. This in turn suggests that the chairman can exploit the friendship-value of the seats next to him.

- There is a "dead man's corner" on the chairman's right, especially if a number of people are seated in line along from him (it does not apply if he is alone at the head of the table).

- As a general rule, proximity to the chairman is a sign of honor and favor. This is most marked when he is at the head of a long, narrow table. The greater the distance, the lower the rank— just as the lower-status positions were "below the salt" at medieval refectories.

Control the garrulous. In most meetings someone takes a long time to say very little. As chairman, your sense of urgency should help indicate to him the need for brevity. You can also suggest that if he is going to take a long time it might be better for him to write a paper. If it is urgent to stop him in full flight, there is a useful device of picking on a phrase (it really doesn't matter what phrase) as he utters it as an excuse for cutting in and offering it to someone else: "Inevitable decline—that's very interesting. George, do you agree that the decline is inevitable?"

Draw out the silent. In any properly run meeting, as simple arithmetic will show, most of the people will be silent most of the time. Silence can indicate general agreement, or no important contribution to make, or the need to wait and hear more before saying anything or too good a lunch, and none of these need worry you. But there are two kinds of silence you must break:

1. **The silence of diffidence.** Someone may have a valuable contribution to make but be sufficiently nervous about its possible reception to keep it to himself. It is important that when you draw out such a contribution, you should express interest and pleasure (though not necessarily agreement) to encourage further contributions of that sort.

2. **The silence of hostility.** This is not hostility to ideas, but to you as the chairman, to the meeting, and to the process by which decisions are being reached.

This sort of total detachment from the whole proceedings is usually the symptom of some feeling of affront. If you probe it, you will usually find that there is something bursting to come out, and that it is better out than in.

Protect the weak. Junior members of the meeting may provoke the disagreement of their seniors, which is perfectly reasonable. But if the disagreement escalates to the point of suggesting that they have no right to contribute, the meeting is weakened. So you may have to

take pains to commend their contribution for its useful-
ness, as a pre-emptive measure. You can reinforce this
action by taking a written note of a point they make
(always a plus for a member of a meeting) and by referring to it again later in the discussion (a double-plus).

Encourage the clash of ideas. But, at the same time,
discourage the clash of personalities. A good meeting is
not a series of dialogues between individual members
and the chairman. Instead, it is a crossflow of discussion
and debate, with the chairman occasionally guiding,
meditating, probing, stimulating, and summarizing, but
mostly letting the others thrash *ideas* out. However, the
meeting must be a contention of ideas, not people.
    If two people are starting to get heated, widen the
discussion by asking a question of a neutral member of
the meeting, preferably a question that requires a purely
factual answer.

Watch out for the suggestion-squashing reflex.
Students of meetings have reduced everything that can
be said into questions, answers, positive reactions, and
negative reactions. Questions can only seek, and answers
only supply, three types of responses: information, opinion, and suggestion.
    In almost every modern organization, it is the sugges-
tions that contain the seeds of future success. Although
very few suggestions will ever lead to anything, almost
all of them need to be given every chance. The trouble is
that suggestions are much easier to ridicule than facts or
opinions. If people feel that making a suggestion will
provoke the negative reaction of being laughed at or
squashed, they will soon stop. And if there is any status-
jostling going on at the meeting, it is all too easy to use

the occasion of someone's making a suggestion as the opportunity to take him down a peg. It is all too easy and a formula to ensure sterile meetings.

The answer is for you to take special notice and show special warmth when anyone makes a suggestion, and to discourage as sharply as you can the squashing-reflex. This can often be achieved by requiring the squasher to produce a better suggestion on the spot. Few suggestions can stand up to squashing in their pristine state: your reflex must be to pick out the best part of one and get the other committee members to help build it into something that might work.

Come to the most senior people last. Obviously, this cannot be a rule, but once someone of high authority has pronounced on a topic, the less senior members are likely to be inhibited. If you work up the pecking order instead of down it, you are apt to get a wider spread of views and ideas. But the juniors who start it off should only be asked for contributions within their personal experience and competence ("Peter, you were at the Frankfurt Exhibition—what reactions did you pick up there?").

Close on a note of achievement. Even if the final item is left unresolved, you can refer to an earlier item that was well resolved as you close the meeting and thank the group.

If the meeting is not a regular one, fix the time and place of the next one before dispersing. A little time spent with appointment diaries at the end, especially if it is a gathering of five or more members, can save hours of secretarial telephoning later.

FOLLOWING THE MEETING

Your secretary may take the minutes (or better still, one of the members), but the minutes are your responsibility. They can be very brief, but they should include these facts:

- The time and date of the meeting, where it was held, and who chaired it.

- Names of all present and apologies for absence.

- All agenda items (and other items) discussed and all decisions reached. If action was agreed on, record (and underline) the name of the person responsible for the assignment.

- The time at which the meeting ended (important, because it may be significant later to know whether the discussion lasted 15 minutes or 6 hours).

- The date, time, and place of the next committee meeting.

Originally published in March–April 1976
Reprint 76204

Creative Meetings through Power Sharing

GEORGE M. PRINCE

Executive Summary

DIALOGUES AMONG PERSONS, where there is a
superior-subordinate relationship, are usually characterized by an implicit recognition of the superior's authority.
Whether or not he exercises that authority, all present
are aware that the superior can reward or punish their
actions. So, rather than speaking freely and frankly, the
subordinates become conditioned to participating in a
manner calculated to win his approval. The author
examines the dynamics of meetings, showing how the
behavior of participants can stifle initiative and inhibit the
free exchange of ideas. He suggests a different
approach, in which managers spur the expression of
constructive ideas by sharing their power and acting as
collaborators with their subordinates.

Meetings are obviously an important part of a manager's life. In face-to-face encounters with one or more of his subordinates or peers, problems are brought up, information is shared, presentations are made, new ideas are developed, and, often, decisions are made.

One would think that meetings are an exciting and rewarding component of business life. But this is the case far too seldom. Most meetings are notable for hidden agendas, lack of candor, and waste of talent. This produces a high level of frustration and boredom for participants and a low level of accomplishment, both for the company and for those persons present. (See "Nature of Conference Process" at the end of this article.)

One reason why meetings so often seem to accomplish so little—and by "meeting" I am thinking particularly of a gathering involving two or more persons where there is a superior-subordinate relationship—is that those present never forget that the organization's system of reward and punishment is still operating. To put it more precisely, the manager (the superior) does not let them forget.

Most managers operate with a style that I call judgmental. It is characterized by an emphasis on the power and right of the manager to pass judgment on actions of his subordinates.

The manager may keep hands off as subordinates prepare proposals for presentation to him. Such useful devices as delegation of authority, management by objectives, and participative management attempt to augment the autonomy of the subordinate, but meaningful decisions are usually reserved to managers well up the corporate ladder. In fact, one's right to make important decisions is the single most telling measure of status and power.

As a result, there is heavy emphasis on getting and guarding the power to decide important issues. This view of power as the right to make decisions about and comment more or less freely on actions, ideas, and proposals of subordinates puts the manager in a judgmental posture.

But as a judgmental manager he places himself in a difficult situation: if he maintains detachment in order to be fair to his subordinates, he removes himself somewhat from the action. On the other hand, if he uses his experience and skills in the usual way to involve himself in the discussion leading up to the decision to be made, he becomes a partisan. Then he is competing with his subordinates rather than playing his superior role as a manager/decision maker. In either case, much of the satisfaction of cooperative accomplishment is denied him.

In practice, the manager often walks a devious middle path. He uses persuasion and informal rewards and punishments to lead his subordinates to propose only what he can decide on favorably. But they resent his manipulation of them if they realize it. The result is misunderstanding and suspicion that make wholehearted cooperation difficult.

In my view, there is a better way of dealing with subordinates in order to obtain cooperation and further the organization's goals. But the better way cannot be imposed from above; it requires a collaborative effort between superiors and subordinates. I shall describe an approach to establishing a climate that encourages new ideas and innovation.

Conditioned Responses

An organization's informal reward and punishment system is less visible than the formal one of salaries, bonuses, and promotions, but no less real. It is based on the tacit dependence of subordinate on superior. Each subordinate must often—perhaps several times a day—try to guess what action will be acceptable to his manager. To win acceptance rather than suffer rejection, he soon becomes conditioned to anticipating how his boss will react to an idea or a proposal.

On the face of it, this appears to be a good way for a subordinate to learn how to perform well in his job. In fact, it has a quite different effect, because it stifles initiative and leads to organizational inertia. This condition can create rather ludicrous situations, such as this case:

> *The marketing vice president of a company was asked why he did not make himself more available to his sales managers, so that they could benefit from his considerable talent and experience. "The problem is," he said, "that they listen to me too hard. For instance, I'll be just speculating that a red can might increase shelf visibility and suddenly the cans are red."*

Nearly every manager will deny that he conditions his subordinates. But he should ask himself whether *his* manager lets him forget the superior-subordinate relationship and his explicit power to pass judgment on ideas and recommendations presented to him.

Let me make it clear that I believe controls and guidance to be appropriate and necessary. What concerns me is the destructive conditioning that pervades our organizational climate.

The hierarchical organization makes such apparent sense and has been so productive that it is hard to recognize the destructiveness of this manipulative force. But talk candidly to younger managers and you will observe that they—and, increasingly, older managers too—are very vocal in their frustration over the "Mickey Mouse" methods that corporations employ in the name of efficiency and the welfare of the organization.

Rejection and Approval

If you could watch and listen to video and sound tapes of business meetings, you would note the pervasiveness of the judgmental managerial style in corporate life. In watching and listening to hundreds of these tapes over many years, I have been impressed again and again by these observations:

- Even mild rejection has a significant negative effect on people.

- Pointing out flaws in the ideas and actions of others occupies much of the time.

- Approval has a positive effect on people and creates a climate for resolution of the problem.

In this section I shall discuss these phenomena in terms of business meetings.

EFFECTS OF REJECTION

There is a widespread belief that in maturity one learns to take the slings and arrows of fortune with equanimity. And to some extent this is true. As one matures, he becomes more philosophical and learns to keep in perspective the daily ups and downs that occur.

One also learns to conceal his true feelings from others. While hurt feelings may not surface at all, more often they are translated unconsciously into uncooperative or even aggressive behavior aimed at the person who has stepped on one's toes. In a meeting, such action is usually disguised as a rational and potentially useful contribution to the dialogue. It is considered mature to view such behavior in this light, so it is easy to forget how sensitive to rejection mature people are.

Let us study the effects of rejection by dissecting the interaction that takes place at a meeting. (To illustrate more clearly my points about rejection and acceptance, I shall not include a superior-subordinate relationship here, but in a later vignette.) Let us suppose a group of four is working to improve one of their company's products, the familiar director's chair, which consists of a wooden frame and two slings.

Mr. First: *Let's replace the canvas with nylon.*

This is an *offer.* Its chief characteristics are that it contains information and (sometimes or) an idea. More important for our purposes, the person who makes it gets a feeling of worth and satisfaction from it.

Mr. Second: *I think that's a good idea because it will give us better weathering characteristics.*

This is an *acceptance.* It conveys credit and approval to the offerer and gives a reason why the idea merits approval. The originator of an acceptance tends to get pleasure from this action. In addition, the acceptance reinforces Mr. First's feeling of worth and satisfaction. He also views Mr. Second as an ally and a man of taste and perception—a person to pay attention to.

Mr. Third: *Will nylon take the bright dyes that we use?*

This is a *query*, and it is a slippery, chameleonlike element. A friendly query is perceived by Mr. First, the offerer, as clearly seeking information. He sifts words, tone, and nonverbal signals to determine whether this is a friendly query. If he perceives it to be so, he retains his positive feelings and speculates comfortably and openly with Mr. Third. If, however, he considers the query unfriendly, it constitutes a *rejection* and he reacts defensively or perhaps aggressively. Participants in a dialogue often use questions to make an offerer either defend his contribution or see the folly of it.

Mr. Fourth: *That's a good idea, First, but nylon will stretch much more than canvas and the user will hit the supports.*

This is another kind of rejection. What appears at the start to be an acceptance proves to be just sugarcoating of the pill. The chief characteristic of a rejection is its negativeness. Regardless of how politely conveyed and how factually accurate and even necessary this negative information is, the offerer perceives it as a put-down. His sense of worth and satisfaction is injured.

The feelings of the rejector are mixed. Even if the information he offers in support of his rejection is important and necessary, the satisfaction of giving it is eroded by the knowledge that he has used his information to put someone else down.

Punishment and backlash. Nearly everything that happens in conversation can be described in terms of these elements. There are thousands of ways to reject. Through use of the proper (or improper) tone an acceptance or query can be turned into a flat rejection. For example, a question such as "Are you seriously suggesting we do that?" is clearly a rejection. The same can be accomplished by a countersuggestion, silence, changing the subject, and countless other actions, many of them nonverbal.

In a meeting of several people, typically about half of the transactions involve rejections. In the rough-and-tumble of the usual discussion, many of the rejections pass unnoticed. If one asks a participant if he perceived some negative action toward him as a rejection, he will nearly always say *no*. We are all thoroughly conditioned to appear to accept rejection, since that is considered to be mature behavior.

Often a participant is unaware that he is hurt and angry over a rejection. But if he is carefully observed, his nonverbal reactions may tell a different story. The signals are faint: an animated face turns into a poker face, the arms cross, or the head jerks backward slightly.

Better evidence may come later, if the rejected offerer tries to justify his offer or pay back his adversary in kind, rather than responding to the substance of the rejection. Let us continue the dialogue.

Mr. Fourth: *I have an idea! We could double over this part of the fabric and—*

Mr. First: *That would increase our costs too much.*

Mr. First rejects Mr. Fourth's idea before he can possibly know what Mr. Fourth has in mind.

The most important aspect of a rejection is the transformation of any transaction or exchange from potentially rewarding to punishing. If a manager is unaware of the dynamics of his transactions, he will tend to rely heavily on pointing out flaws or presenting countersuggestions. Both of these are usually perceived as rejections. So the manager is unintentionally punishing and conditioning subordinates to offer ideas or take action very cautiously—if at all.

POINTING OUT FLAWS

In meetings called to attack particular problems, this sequence can be repeatedly observed: one member suggests an idea containing some elements that will help solve the problem. It is not, however, a completely acceptable solution. The manager and the other participants focus on the failings of idea and firmly point them out. The group discards it to search for a new and better idea.

This series of reactions is considered rational and useful because ideas are judged good and worth pursuing or unhelpful and weeded out quickly. Time is not wasted on ideas that cannot stand up to this early testing.

The flaw in this reasoning has become apparent in an experiment which I have conducted hundreds of times with different groups. Of, say, ten groups working to solve the same difficult problem, nine fail to develop a concept to solve it. The tenth considers an idea discarded by the other nine and is intrigued by it, although it fails to meet some of the specifications of the problem. The group struggles with these shortcomings and somehow, making modifications as it goes along, transforms the bad idea into a good one that meets the specifications.

In analyzing the results of this reiterated experiment, I have pinpointed seven ideas that are regularly weeded out and discarded because they fail the early testing. Yet each of these unacceptable ideas can be transformed into an acceptable solution, and has been by the odd group (about one in ten) that becomes interested in it and struggles cooperatively to overcome its weaknesses.

While watching video tapes of these experiments, I have observed how often members of a group choose to focus on the flaws of an idea rather than on overcoming the flaws. The evidence from one incident, or several, might lead one to conclude, "Pointing out a flaw is the first step in overcoming it." This can, of course, be true. But when, in thousands of incidents, the second step seldom follows, one questions the benign intent behind pointing out a flaw.

One can then identify other evidence that suggests that this behavior serves some other purpose: the tone of voice may be unfriendly and may be accompanied by expressions or gestures that indicate disdain, impatience, or satisfaction in catching the offerer in sloppy thinking. Very seldom does pointing out a flaw convey helpful concern.

What other purpose does it serve? I believe that such behavior is an attempt to exercise power over another person. Implicit is the notion that one's co-workers are adversaries in an unending competition, and that one wins (or at least cuts his losses) by rendering someone else's idea worthless. The manager is not exempt from these feelings. When he is operating with subordinates, however, his stakes are much lower; he can always win.

CLIMATE OF APPROVAL

The beginning of improvement in conditions comes when the manager recognizes that for productivity's sake, at least, he must avoid transactions between individuals that arouse defensive or revengeful reactions. Instead, he must establish a climate in which it is appropriate to voice imperfect thoughts and ideas. In this climate all ideas are explored and used by the group. Flaws are dealt with, but as drawbacks to be overcome by everyone.

In my experience, when this climate is present, rejections, unfriendly queries, and pointing-out-a-flaw behavior are practically eliminated. Idea production rises dramatically. Every idea is noted and explored to some extent. According to the participants, they often come out of these meetings feeling exhilarated, pleased with having made worthwhile contributions, and sometimes even personally enriched.

The concrete results of this style of meeting are more difficult to evaluate. The participants consistently rate this type of meeting as more productive and useful than a traditional meeting. But one cannot quantify solutions to problems per meeting; the most important results emerge gradually out of the clarifying effect of disciplined cooperation. These results take the form of more frequent individual and group accomplishment and increased satisfaction and motivation.

The Judicious Manager

Since there are so many drawbacks to judgmental management, why does anyone use this style? I suggested
earlier that in our culture there is little apparent choice.
Given the heavy emphasis on productivity and profit, it
appears that an effective manager must use his power to
govern important matters.

Another limiting factor in choice of styles is a lack of
models. Among one's teachers, managers, peers, and
subordinates, it is difficult to find someone who is not
judgmental.

Also, the fact that this style tends to be punishing to
subordinates may even reinforce its use. As Walter Nord
says, "Punishment is the most widely used technique in
our society for behavior control."[1] He goes on to suggest
that because punishment immediately stops the unde-
sired response, the punisher is rewarded or reinforced
for punishing. If negativeness and pointing out a flaw
are seen as punishing, one can understand the manager's attraction to a judgmental posture.

The kind of manager who, in contrast, relies on affir-
mation and collaboration to get results I call the judicious manager. He holds different assumptions about
power, efficiency, roles, and decision making. The con-
trasting assumptions are summarized in the table "Con-
trasting the Assumptions of a Judgmental Manager and
a Judicious Manager." (These propositions owe much to
Abraham Maslow, Douglas McGregor, Gordon Lippitt,
and the other giants of humanistic psychology.)

Obviously, I am not discussing merely managerial
styles, but attitudes toward others and how people interact. People are quite consistent in the ways they act; the
strategies one uses in a meeting tend to be the same as

Contrasting the Assumptions of a Judgmental Manager and a Judicious Manager

Judgmental Manager	Judicious Manager
The most efficient mode is to have one boss call the shots.	The most efficient mode is to make use cooperatively of the varied talents available.
I must protect my power to make decisions.	The best decision will emerge if I combine my power with that of the implementers.
I decide every course of action where I am authorized to decide.	I enlist my subordinates to devise courses of action, and contribute my thoughts as matters progress.
I must exercise all the autonomy my power permits.	I must use my power to help each subordinate develop his or her autonomy.
I use my power for my own growth.	I share my power so that my subordinates can grow as I grow.
I motivate people.	Accomplishment motivates people. I can provide opportunities for accomplishment.
I review, oversee, and control the efforts of my subordinates.	I use my experience, power, and skill to aid subordinates in accomplishing the task.
I take credit for the results of the groups I manage.	I explicitly recognize the accomplishments of subordinates.
To get results I must spot flaws and have them corrected.	To get results we must help each other overcome flaws.
When subordinates express themselves or act in ways unacceptable to me, I point out the flaws.	When subordinates express themselves or act in unacceptable ways, I assume they had reasons that made sense to them and explore the action from that point of view.
As mature people we are able to "take" put-downs and criticism without destructive consequences.	Even mature people are distressed to some degree by put-downs and criticism, and this makes cooperation difficult.
My role is to define the mission of my group.	My role in mission definition is to facilitate discovery by my subordinates and myself.
My role is to make judgments about the actions of my subordinates while they are carrying out our mission.	My role is to join my subordinates to make sure they succeed.

those one uses in other situations. For example, a manager who uses humor to try to soften his criticism of ideas and behavior in a meeting probably does the same in any situation where he exercises power over others. A manager who uses questions in meetings to mask his rejections does the same in other contexts.

Changing from a system of informal punishment and rewards is difficult because of the confusions in our present judgmental system. For example, autonomy and cooperation may seem antithetical. In reality they are not. The autonomous person has less need to be defensive and competitive and is therefore free to use his power to appreciate, support, and build on the action or idea of another.

Situations and people are changing continuously. Each of us has bad days, makes mistakes, and some days is less able to cope. Misunderstanding and confusion are an everyday part of this reality. That is why the manager must carry on a continuous clarification of roles and expectations.

Recognize Others' Value

Meetings provide an ideal way of carrying out this mission. The best way of using the meeting to redefine roles and expectations is to tape-record them (video tape is best, if available, but sound tape is satisfactory too). It is too difficult to reconstruct the fast action of a meeting without having a tape of it. Later the participants can analyze the tape. Thus each member of the group can take his turn analyzing parts where he made offers.

To illustrate, I shall analyze a simple episode, in which a manager and two subordinates at a food-processing company are discussing how they might reduce shipping costs.

Mr. A: *You know, if we decentralize our manufacturing, we could cut shipping costs.*

Mr. B: *A more practical way would be to get some more competition among our carriers.*

Manager: *You remember we had a dispute with AA Trucking about eight months ago and got some bids from others. It would be worth examining that possibility again.*

The following pluses and minuses can be identified in this exchange:

Plus—Two different offers were quickly forthcoming.

Plus—Everyone is focusing on an aspect of the same problem.

Plus—The manager accepted one.

Minus—Mr. A's offer is rejected when the others ignore it.

Minus—Mr. B suggests that Mr. A is not practical.

Minus—The manager puts subordinates in a competitive, win-lose position.

The next step is for the group to take each minus, rephrase it as a problem, and come up with a solution. Let us consider the problem of how to avoid rejection of Mr. A's offer. The manager wants to encourage idea generation, but his action has the opposite effect on Mr. A. Though the manager knows that he should acknowledge every offer and assume that the idea it contains has some value, he gave it short shrift.

Why? From the little evidence we have here, it appears that the manager heard two offers almost at once, which, of course, often happens in meetings. He evidently selected the one that seemed more realistic to him in light of the company's experience. But what seemed to him to be perfectly reasonable action was to Mr. A arbitrary rejection of his idea, without enlightenment as to the manager's grounds.

So we note a discrepancy between the manager's perception of the episode and Mr. A's. Such discrepancies lead to misunderstanding and confusion. The victim wastes energy in speculating about their meaning or, worse, feels resentful and, perhaps unconsciously, determines to "get even."

A useful procedure for avoiding rejections is based on the assumption that an idea made some sort of sense to the person who expressed it—no matter what flaws leaped immediately to the listener's mind. So the burden is on the listener to speculate first about the useful aspects of the idea.

Only after exercising his wit and imagination on the constructive elements may he air his concerns or speak of flaws he sees. Even then, if he can word his concerns and flaws as subproblems to be worked on, he will keep the group's energy focused on building a solution.

Here is how the shipping-cost meeting might go if everyone knew and used this technique.

Mr. A: *You know, if we decentralize our manufacturing, we could cut shipping costs.*

Manager: *Decentralizing would do some nice things for us. It* would *save on shipping and it would give us smaller, faster-moving manufacturing units. Another* *thing I like about the idea is that it would break up this huge, centralized operation and spread responsibilities in the organization.* (Having acknowledged the value in Mr. A's thinking and revealed some of his values too, the manager shifts to his own concerns.) *I have some problems here to consider—how to decentralize without any capital expense, for one. Another is how to retain both economies of scale and the advantages of small plants.*

Mr. B: *I have an idea about keeping capital expenses down. We could take a whole packing line and farm it out to someone in the area we want to operate in. We could contract with him to work for us on an exclusive basis.*

Manager: *Yeah, that would get around the capital problem—we might lease the equipment to a supplier—and it would get us out from under the production problems. It also puts the emphasis on our marketing strengths, where we are superior. But I have a couple of concerns here. How do we persuade the chairman—you know how he loves the production end—and how do we maintain quality control?*

Mr. A: *What this suggests to me is that we might keep production here and control it as usual—just condense our stews and soups and have reconstituting or repackaging stations at decentralized locations.*

Manager: *Sure, we could ship the condensed product in tank cars and just decentralize our packaging. I like this line of thought. Perhaps we wouldn't even have to condense if we were using bulk shipping. Now let's see, we* *have two things to explore, the condense-and-reconstitute idea and the bulk shipment with decentralized packaging. Anyone have any other approaches?*

Another way of recognizing value in subordinates and of clarifying expectations is to delegate the decision making to the one who is to be the direct implementer of the undertaking. The purpose of the meeting (or a portion of it) is to provide him with alternatives. The manager must take care to maintain his participatory role and to avoid taking over the decision making. If he has concerns about an alternative being developed, he should state first what is useful in the developing idea and then turn to the problems he sees.

Finally, the subordinate selects among the alternatives. He may select an alternative which the manager considers acceptable but not the best one available. At times like these the manager proves his mettle. Accepting the subordinate's decision is not easy, since he knows that the ultimate responsibility is his. He may be asked by *his* boss to account for the results of a "second best" decision. However, a judicious manager knows that this is the risk he must repeatedly take if his subordinates are to grow in commitment and autonomy.

In these ways the manager can make a profound change in how he is perceived. He is relying on his experience and wisdom, not to judge and impose the accept-reject alternatives, but to encourage, teach, guide, and capitalize on the powers of his subordinates. He is very much into and a part of the action. Meetings can become a place where there are many rewards for the offering and few punishments.

Concluding Note

Dealing with problems is the everyday job of a manager. By shifting from the judgmental to the judicious mode, the manager frees himself to contribute all his skill, experience, and knowledge without relegating subordinates to the position of lackeys. In doing this, he does not relinquish his responsibilities of guidance and control.

In short, the judicious manager enjoys his job more is while he makes a much larger contribution and helps his subordinates do the same.

Nature of Conference Process

FOR A YOUNG MAN ON THE MAKE there is no better vehicle than the conference way. Where fifty years before he might have had to labor unseen by all but his immediate superior, now via the conference he can expose himself to all sorts of superiors across the line of command. Given minimum committeemanship skills, by an adroit question here and a modest suggestion there, he can call attention to himself and still play the game.

But as he succeeds in the struggle he comes into contact more and more with the frustrating nature of the process. He is, let it be noted, very, very good at team playing—he wouldn't have risen if he wasn't. But more and more he begins to see the other side of the coin of "multiple management." He still presents the equable facade—he listens as if he really liked to and suggests rather than orders—and he half persuades himself that he is just suggesting. But down underneath, that ego is hardening.

The executive is very gregarious when he sees some practical utility to the gregariousness. But if he doesn't see that utility, good fellowship bores him to death. One of the most recurring notes in executives' complaints about their work loads is the uselessness of so much of the socializing they have to put up with—whether it is entertaining after hours or human relations during hours. One rather studious executive, who at the time was bucking for a vice-presidency, put it this way: "It is when you get where I am that you see the difference between the 'contributory' and the 'noncontributory' aspects of the job. You've got to endure a tremendous mount of noncontributory labor—this talking back and forth, and meetings, and so on. The emptiness and the frustration of it can be appalling. But you've got to put up with it, there's no mistake about that, and you just hope that you can keep your eye on the contributory phases which put you on the glory road."[2]

Notes

1. "Beyond the Teaching Machine: The Neglected Area of Operant Conditioning in the Theory and Practice of Management," *Organizational Behavior and Human Performance*, Vol. 4, 1969, p. 383.

2. William H. Whyte, Jr., *The Organization Man*, New York, Simon & Schuster, Inc., 1956, pp. 152–153. Copyright © 1956 by William H. Whyte, Jr. Reprinted with permission of William H. Whyte, Jr.

Originally published in July–August 1972
Reprint 72410

Nobody Trusts the Boss Completely—Now What?

FERNANDO BARTOLOMÉ

Executive Summary

CATCHING PROBLEMS EARLY is a big advantage to
any manager, and the best way to find out about developing headaches is to have your subordinates tell you.
But how do you get them to be candid? How do you
get to talk freely about their own mistakes—and, harder
yet, about yours?

Candor depends on trust. Both have strict natural limits. People keep their mouths shut in order to protect
themselves or their subordinates, to avoid the limelight,
or because they are afraid of seeming timid or ineffec-
tual, and so they try to fix their own problems without
help. Company politics can also stand in the way of
plain talk. Worst of all, trust avoids authority and flees a
judge. Since employees always see the boss as judge,
managers need to be aware of how they can increase
trust—or destroy it. There are six critical areas:

1. **Communication** must always be a two-way street.

2. **Support** means being approachable, helpful, and concerned, especially when the chips are down.

3. **Respect** is a question of delegating authority and listening to what subordinates have to say.

4. **Fairness** means giving credit and assessing blame where they are due.

5. **Predictability** is being dependable and keeping promises.

6. **Competence** means knowing your own job and doing it well.

But given the limits of trust, good managers watch for other telltale signs of trouble: decline in the information flow, deteriorating morale, ambiguous verbal messages, nonverbal signals, and diminishing results. Once these signs are recognized, managers need techniques for amplifying hints and gathering supplemental information. The key is a communication network based on properly using, spreading, and creating information.

MANAGERS WHO CAN head off serious problems before they blow up in the company's face are two steps ahead of the game. Their employers avoid needless expense or outright disaster, and they themselves get the promotions they deserve for running their departments smoothly and nipping trouble neatly in the bud.

In practice, of course, it's never this easy. Everyone knows that one trick to dealing with problems is to learn about them early. But what's the trick to learning about them early? How do effective managers find out that trouble is brewing? What are their warning systems?

All good managers have their own private information networks, and many develop a kind of sixth sense for the early signs of trouble. But by far the simplest and most common way to find out about problems is to be told, usually by a subordinate.

It is easy to get information when things are going well. People love to give the boss good news. But subordinates are never eager to tell their supervisors that the latest scheme isn't working, to assume ownership of a problem by giving it a name, to look like an informer, or to sound like Chicken Little. A subordinate's reluctance to be frank about problems is also related to risk. While it's fairly easy to tell the boss that the machines sent over by the purchasing department aren't working properly, it's much harder to admit responsibility for the malfunction, and harder still—and perhaps dangerous—to blame it on the boss. Yet it is terribly important to get subordinates to convey unpleasant messages. The sooner a problem is disclosed, diagnosed, and corrected, the better for the company.

Subordinates are never eager to give the boss bad news.

Almost any organization would operate more effectively with completely open and forthright employees, but absolute frankness is too much to hope for (and probably too much to bear). Candor depends upon trust, and in hierarchical organizations, trust has strict natural limits.

The Limits of Trust and Candor

In a hierarchy, it is natural for people with less power to be extremely cautious about disclosing weaknesses, mistakes, and failings—especially when the more powerful party is also in a position to evaluate and punish. Trust flees authority, and, above all, trust flees a judge. Managers are inescapably positioned to judge subordinates. Good managers may be able to confine evaluation to formal occasions, to avoid all trace of judgmental style in other settings, even to communicate criticism in a positive, constructive way. But there is no way to escape completely a subordinate's inclination to see superiors as judges.

So one of the limits on candor is self-protection. For example, people often hide the failures of their own departments and hope they will correct themselves. In one typical case, the development group for a piece of special software fell terribly behind on its schedule, but no one told the manager until the delivery date could no longer be met. Delivery was three months late, and the company had to absorb a financial penalty.

The lack of candor was not self-protective in the long run, of course, because the development group was ultimately held responsible for the delay. But human beings are often shortsighted. At one time or another, most of us have chosen an uncertain future calamity over today's immediate unpleasantness.

A variation on this theme is when subordinates protect their own subordinates in order to protect themselves, as in the following example:

I was vice president of finance for a large manufacturing company and supervised a staff of 27. One new hire was failing on an important assignment. Her supervisor—who had hired her—withheld this information from me until her failure could no longer be corrected without serious disruption. He didn't tell me because he knew I would make him face up to the problem and deal with it, which he knew he would find very difficult to do.

Sometimes a subordinate may try to protect a client. In one case, a salesman withheld the information that one of his largest customers was in financial trouble. The customer went bankrupt, and the company lost $500,000.

We can only guess at the salesman's motives—eagerness to get his commission before the troubled company failed, fear of losing an old customer, reluctance to give official warning of a danger that might be exaggerated. The fact remains that he failed to communicate the problem, his boss saw no sign of danger, and the company lost half a million dollars.

Often the motive for silence is at least superficially praiseworthy: people keep quiet about a developing problem while trying to solve it. Most believe solving problems on their own is what they're paid to do, and in many cases, they're right. Subordinates are not paid to run to their bosses with every glitch and hiccup. As problems grow more serious, however, managers need to know about them.

The difficulty here lies in the bewildering territory between minor snags and major disasters. Handled promptly and decisively, the problems in this gray area sometimes turn out to be insignificant, but self-confident supervisors, particularly inexperienced ones, are perhaps too eager to prove they can cope on their own. This case is typical:

> *I am head of medical research in a pharmaceutical company. My job is part of R&D and is on the critical path to marketing any new product. One of my managers saw that we weren't receiving data critical to the timely generation of a licensing package for worldwide registration of a new drug. He spent four months trying to get the data on his own, or proceed without it, and didn't inform me of the problem. We suffered an eight-month delay in applying for a license to sell. That represents 10% of the patent life of the product, which has estimated peak worldwide sales of $120 million a year.*

Politics is another common obstacle to candor. Organizations are political systems, and employees are often involved in political struggles. There is no guarantee your subordinates will be on your side.

A U.S. engineering-products company manufactured a successful product on license from a Swedish company, but the American CEO heartily disliked his Swedish counterpart and came to the private conclusion that the licensing fees were out of line. Knowing that his senior staff would object, he began confidential acquisition talks with one of the Swedish corporation's competitors, a much smaller and technically less sophisticated company. Because the negotiations were too complex for him to handle alone, he circumvented the vice presidents who would have opposed the move and secretly enlisted the help of their subordinates. By the

Mergers, acquisitions, and office politics can all choke off the flow of essential information.

time the negotiations became public, it was too late for the senior staff to stop the deal. The Swedish company canceled its license, and the U.S. company has not sold a single piece of new technology since the acquisition.

This CEO made a grave error in letting his personal feelings interfere with his business judgment, but his incompetence, however great, is not the point. The point is that certain employees concealed information from their immediate superiors. Their motives are easy to guess at and perhaps understandable—after all, they were acting on orders from the CEO. But the fact remains that not one of them spoke up, their superiors suspected nothing, and the consequences for the company were extremely negative.

In these days of mergers and acquisitions, political infighting is often acute after absorption of—or by—another company. Restructuring and consolidation can produce epidemic fear and rupture lines of communication, as this case illustrates:

My electronics corporation acquired a division of another company and merged it with two existing subsidiaries. Many employees were let go in the process of the merger and consolidation. I was named president and CEO of the new company one year after its formation. The new company had its headquarters on the East Coast and its research facilities in the West. The VP for research—whose office was in California—did not tell me that the merger, the layoffs, and the new company policies and procedures had had a terrible impact on employee morale. I was completely unaware of the problem for four months. Then I visited the research facility to announce a new benefits package. After announcing the plan, I asked for questions. All hell broke loose. For the next year and a half I spent about a third of my time and a great deal of other people's time trying to build bridges and establish trust, hoping to lower turnover, improve productivity, and get those Californians to feel like part of the total company.

Why wasn't I told? My guess is that the subordinate who kept me in the dark was afraid for his own job. Or else he felt he had something to gain by undermining my position. I don't know, but it was an expensive failure of communication.

Building and Destroying Trust

Given the natural obstacles to trust and candor—fear, pride, politics, dislike—managers need to make the most of whatever opportunities they have to increase subordinates' trust. Trust is not easy to build in the best of cases, and the kind of trust that concerns us here has to grow on rocky ground—between people at different levels of authority.

Resist the temptation to use information as a tool or a reward.

The factors affecting the development of trust and candor fall into six categories: communication, support, respect, fairness, predictability, and competence.

Communication is a matter of keeping subordinates informed, providing accurate feedback, explaining decisions and policies, being candid about one's own problems, and resisting the temptation to hoard information for use as a tool or a reward.

For several years, the founder and CEO of a small, South American conglomerate had addressed the needs of each of his six divisions separately. He treated his vice presidents like the CEOs of the divisions, cutting deals with each of them independently and keeping each in the dark about his arrangements with the others. He had always solved problems on this ad hoc basis, and it worked reasonably well. The company had grown swiftly and steadily. But now times were tougher, the company was bigger, and he began getting complaints from his VPs about resource allocation. None of them was satisfied with his own division's share, but none was in a position to consider the needs of the company as a whole. At this point, the CEO recognized that his way of managing was part of the problem, did an abrupt about-face, and created an executive committee comprising himself and his six VPs. They all took part in setting priorities, allocating resources, and planning company strategy. Conflicts remained, of course, as each vice president fought for resources for his division. But trust increased substantially, and for the first time there was communication between divisions and a willingness and opportunity for the company's leadership to work together as a team.

Another CEO moved the offices of his small company without notice. His staff simply arrived at work one Monday morning to learn that the movers were coming on Tuesday. When asked to explain, the man gave his reasons but clearly didn't feel his employees needed to know. He insulted and belittled the people he depended on for information and support.

It is important to communicate with subordinates not only as a group but also as individuals. This woman's boss may have believed money spoke for itself:

> *I have been working for my current boss for two years and never had a performance appraisal. I guess I'm*

doing okay because I get good raises every year. But I have no idea what the future may hold for me in this company.

Middle- to upper-level managers often find it difficult to talk with superiors about their own performance and career prospects. When they feel they aren't getting the feedback they need, they are uncomfortable asking for it. Communication must flow in both directions if it is to flow at all. Information won't surge up where it barely trickles down.

Support means showing concern for subordinates as people. It means being available and approachable. It means helping people, coaching them, encouraging their ideas, and defending their positions. It may mean socializing with them. It certainly means taking an interest in their lives and careers. Here are three examples of good and poor support:

During one period of my life, I had some serious personal problems that affected my work. My boss protected me at work and gave me a lot of moral support. Eventually, I was able to solve my problems, thanks in part to her help. That strengthened our professional relationship enormously.

I presented a proposal to the executive committee. Some members were in favor, others against. I was so young and nervous, I didn't see how I could possibly convince them I was right. Then my boss took on the defense of my proposal, argued energetically in favor of it, and we won. When I think back on it now, I realize that few events in my career have pleased me more or given me a more genuine sense of gratitude.

*I approved a credit and had been authorized by my boss
to waive certain credit warranties. Then some other people started questioning what I had done and throwing
doubt on my competence. Instead of supporting me, my
boss took the side of my critics.*

It is often tempting to abandon an employee who is
in trouble, out of favor, or simply unpopular, but the
extra effort expended in behalf of such a person can pay
big dividends later. When you have to terminate
employees, the worst possible method is to let them
twist in the wind. Get rid of those you have to get rid of.
Support the others for all you're worth. Subordinates
trust most deeply the superiors they feel will stand by
them when the chips are down.

Respect feeds on itself. The most important form of
respect is delegation, and the second most important is
listening to subordinates and acting on their opinions.
In the first two examples below, the boss shows genuine
respect for the subordinate's judgment and intelligence.
In the third, the relationship actually deteriorates in the
course of the meeting.

*My boss put me in charge of a project. It involved a big
risk for me, but an even bigger risk for her if I failed. I
asked her how she wanted me to do it and who else I
should contact for clearance. She said, "You have free
rein on this. Whatever you do is okay with me."*

*Six years ago, just after I joined the bank, my boss told
me he had decided to buy a company and asked me to
look into it and give him my opinion. I did my homework
and told him I thought it was a bad idea. So he eliminated me from the team he had put together to manage*

the acquisition. Somehow I succeeded in persuading him to listen to a fuller presentation of my analysis. He not only took the time, he really listened to my arguments and finally canceled the purchase.

My boss and I agreed that we had to reduce the personnel in my department. I wanted to cut five positions; he wanted to cut eight. I argued my case for an hour. In the end he forced me to cut eight jobs, without even answering my arguments, and I realized he hadn't paid attention to anything I'd said.

In interpersonal relations, the law of reciprocity tends to rule. When supervisors use a lot of fine words about trust and respect but behave disdainfully, subordinates are likely to respond in kind.

Fairness means giving credit where it's due, being objective and impartial in performance appraisals, giving praise liberally. The opposite kind of behavior—favoritism, hypocrisy, misappropriating ideas and accomplishments, unethical

Not giving credit where it's due is hugely destructive of trust.

behavior—is difficult to forgive and hugely destructive of trust. These two examples make the point well:

One of my subordinates had what I thought was a terrific idea, and I told my boss. He agreed and immediately dictated a memo to the division manager outlining the idea and giving full credit where it was due. I learned sometime later that he never sent that memo but substituted another in which he took a good share of the credit for himself—and gave an equal share to me. I not only felt cheated, I felt I had somehow taken part in a plot to cheat the person who had the idea in the first place. It not only destroyed my relationship with that boss, it almost ruined my relationship with my subordinate.

We were involved in a very difficult lawsuit with a former client. The battle lasted four years, and in the end we lost the case before the Supreme Court. When I gave the news to my boss, I was afraid he would take it badly, as a kind of personal failure. But he understood that we lost because of factors completely out of our control, and, instead of criticizing us, he praised our hard work and dedication.

Chronic lack of fairness will dry up trust and candor quickly, but every act of support and fair play will prime the pump.

Predictability is a matter of behaving consistently and dependably and of keeping both explicit and implicit promises. A broken promise can do considerable damage, as this example illustrates:

When my boss hired me, she promised me a percentage of the profits on the project I was to manage. My arrival was delayed, so I took over the project as it was winding down—without any profits to speak of. As soon as I cleaned up the loose ends, I took over a new project that was my responsibility from the outset. I managed it well, and profits were substantial. I felt badly cheated when I was told that my percentage deal applied to the first project only, that I had no such agreement on the second. I complained bitterly, and the company made it right. But it left a bad taste in my mouth, and I left shortly afterward.

Another form of predictability is consistency of character, which is, after all, the best proof of authenticity.

Competence, finally, means demonstrating technical and professional ability and good business sense. Employees don't want to be subordinate to people they see as incompetent. Trust grows from seeds of decent behavior, but it thrives on the admiration and respect that only a capable leader can command.

Learning to Recognize Signs of Trouble

Building trust and candor is a gradual process, a long chain of positive experiences: trusting employees with important assignments, publicly defending their positions and supporting their ideas, showing candor and fairness in evaluating their work, and so forth. And because trust takes time to build and has natural limits once achieved, it is easy to destroy. Betraying a confidence, breaking a promise, humiliating an employee in public, lying, withholding information, or excluding subordinates from groups in which they feel they rightly belong—any of these can do instant and irreparable damage to a trust relationship that has taken months or years to develop.

Given these limitations, can managers rely on subordinates to come forward with problems before they become critical?

The obvious answer is no, not entirely. Honest, forthright communication is the best source of information about problems that managers have, and good ones make the most of it. At the same time, they learn to recognize subtle signs of danger, and they develop and refine alternative sources of information to fill in the gaps. My interviews indicate that there are several important warning signs that managers can look for.

Decline in information flow is often a first sign of trouble. Streams of information suddenly go dry. Subordinates communicate less, express opinions reluctantly, avoid discussions—even meetings. Reports are late, subordinates are more difficult to reach, and follow-up has to be more thorough and deliberate. In this example, the first warning was a series of glib reassurances that didn't quite jibe with reality:

> *I was exploration manager for an oil company in Venezuela. I began to notice that when I asked about one particular project, I got very short and superficial answers assuring me that everything was okay. But there were some contradictory signals. For example, labor turnover in the project was quite high. I had a gut feeling that something was seriously wrong. I contacted the area manager, but he couldn't put his finger on any specific problem. I called the field supervisor and still got no clear answers. I went to the field location and spent two days. Nothing. Then I sent a trustworthy young assistant to work with the field crews for a week, and he uncovered the problem. Local labor subcontractors were bribing the workers, increasing turnover, and taking in a lot of money for supplying replacements. We were not only spending more on labor bounties, we were often working with green hands instead of well-trained workers.*

Deterioration of morale can reveal itself in lack of enthusiasm, reduced cooperation, increased complaints about workload, a tendency to dump more minor problems on the boss's desk. At a more advanced stage, absenteeism starts to rise and aggressive behavior—increased criticism, irritability, finger pointing, and the like—appears.

Ambiguous verbal messages come from subordinates who aren't quite comfortable with the information they are passing on. They may be reluctant to blow a potential problem out of proportion, or they may be testing to see if the door is open for a more serious discussion.

In one example, the head of an R&D lab asked the woman in charge of a large research project how a newly hired scientist was working out. The woman said, "He's very bright, but a bit strange. But he's working very hard and is extremely enthusiastic. He's okay." The boss missed the message. "I'm glad everything's okay" was all he said.

In this case, the woman's answer was a typical sign of trouble in sandwich form—positive, negative, positive. The subordinate who answers this way may simply be testing her boss's attention. When he failed to pick up on the "he's a bit strange" remark, she dropped the matter. Her boss never found out that she felt threatened by the scientist's brilliance and that his prima donna behavior made her angry. The friction between them grew, and she eventually took a job with another division.

Nonverbal signals can take a wide variety of forms, from body language to social behavior to changes in routines and habits.

The director of the international division of a major U.S. bank noticed that his chief of Asian operations had begun to work with his office door closed during his frequent visits to New York. This was unusual behavior: he was a gregarious soul, always available for lunch or a chat, and a closed door was out of character.

After two or three such visits, the director invited

him to lunch to talk business. After a bottle of good wine, the younger man brought up what was really on his mind. He had heard rumors that his name had come up to head the European division—the most prestigious foreign assignment—and that the director had opposed him. The rumors were wrong. In fact, the bank was looking for someone to take the director's job, as he was about to be promoted, and the Asian operations chief was a prime candidate.

Consciously or unconsciously, the man sent a signal by closing his door. The lunch invitation was a non-threatening way of finding out what the signal meant. At the time this took place, business had not yet begun to suffer, but more serious trouble might have erupted if this man had continued to brood over false rumors. This prompt response to a nonverbal signal kept a small problem from growing into a big one.

Body language, incidentally, is easily misinterpreted. Popular books have encouraged many people to believe they are experts, but interpreting body language is risky business. Distress signals may be triggered by events in a person's private life, for example, and have nothing to do with the office. A more prudent approach is to see body language merely as an indication of a potential problem, without jumping to conclusions about what the problem may be.

Outside signals, such as customer complaints and problems spotted by other company divisions, are also clear warnings, but they often come too late. By this time, the trouble has usually reached the stage of impaired results—decreasing productivity, deteriorating quality, dwindling orders, declining numbers. By now the manager has long since failed.

Turning Hints into Information

When experienced managers see changes in the behavior of the people they supervise, they do their best to amplify hints and gather supplemental information.

As I pointed out at the beginning of this article, by far the easiest way of obtaining information is to get it from a subordinate, in plain English. Managers who have built good relationships with their subordinates often rely on this method. When they see the early warning signs of trouble, they ask questions.

As I have stressed, the answers to their questions will be only as honest as subordinates want to and dare to give. In other words, successful questioning depends partly on the level of trust. However, it also depends partly on a manager's ability to peel away superficial and sometimes misleading symptoms, much like the outside layers of an onion. Effective managers have good clinical sense. This man, for example, had a gut feeling that he had not yet reached the core of the problem:

> *My department was responsible for trade with the Far East, and I needed a good manager for China. I found what I thought was the perfect man. He not only knew all the traders but also spoke fluent English, French, Chinese, and Japanese. The new position was a promotion for him in terms of title and meant a big salary increase.*
>
> *For the first year, he worked hard, things went well, and we made a lot of money. At the same time, he started to complain about his salary, arguing that other managers reporting to me and doing the same kind of work were getting 20% more—which was true. I told him he'd already had a 25% increase and that if he contin-*

ued doing well, he could expect further raises over the next couple of years.

Then I began hearing his complaint from third parties all over the Far East. I discussed the matter with him many times, and eventually his salary rose to within 5% of the other managers. But something was still wrong. Then he suddenly got sick and disappeared from the office for two weeks. When he returned, his opening words were about salary.

Over the next couple of months, however, his health continued to deteriorate, and I began to wonder if salary was the real problem after all. I had several long talks with him and finally learned the truth. His deteriorating health was related to the job and the level of responsibility, which was too great for him to handle. He was so anxious that he couldn't sleep and was having problems with his family. As soon as we both understood the cause of his problem, I promised him a different job with less stress and frustration. He immediately became more relaxed and happier with his salary and his life.

The salary issue was only a symptom—a particularly misleading one, since the man was in fact underpaid by comparison with his colleagues. Notice also the escalation of symptoms from complaints to illness and the fact that it took the narrator several discussions to get at the actual truth. His persistence grew from a gut feeling that salary was not the real problem but rather a masking symptom.

When conflicts arise between superiors and subordinates, the most common method of punishing the boss is to withhold information. So the greater the conflict is, the less effective direct questioning will be. Furthermore, if an honest answer means pointing out some of the boss's own shortcomings, almost anyone will think twice.

One way of circumventing this difficulty is to design anonymous forms of communication—suggestion boxes, questionnaires, and performance appraisals of managers by the people who work for them.

One manager took advantage of an odd condition in his office space to coax anonymous information from his staff. The offices were on the ninth and tenth floors of an office building and had two elevators of their own, which every employee rode several times a day. The boss put a bulletin board in each of them and posted frequent notices, including a weekly newsletter about office activities, personnel changes, and industry developments. He then let it be known informally that the bulletin boards were open to everyone—no approvals required—and when the first employee notices appeared, he made a point of leaving them in place for a full week. There were only two rules. First, no clippings from newspapers and magazines—contributions had to be original. Second, nothing tasteless or abusive—but complaints and belly-aching were okay.

The bulletin boards flourished, partly because most people had at least an occasional chance to ride alone and post their own views in private. For a while, there was even an anonymous weekly newspaper that handed out praise and criticism pretty freely and irreverently. It made some people uncomfortable, but it had no more avid reader than the boss, who learned volumes about the problems and views of his staff and organization.

Criticizing the boss's managerial style and professional competence is probably the hardest thing for employees to do. Remember two critical points: First, top performers are the most likely to feel secure enough to criticize, so ask them first. Second, many of your subordinates have learned the hard way that honest negative feedback can be dangerous. Never ask for it unless you are certain you can handle it.

Building Information Networks

There are big differences between consuming, disseminating, and creating information. Effective managers seem to have a talent for all three.

Using information well is primarily a matter of not *misusing* it—of being discreet about its sources, of using it not as a weapon but only as a means of solving problems and improving the quality of work life.

Spreading information well means not spreading gossip but also not hoarding the truth. People in organizations want—and have a right to—information that will help them do their jobs better or otherwise affect their lives. In general, they also work better and suffer less stress and fewer complications when they are well informed. At the same time—and more important for this discussion—information attracts information. Managers who are generous with what they know seem to get as much as they give.

Creating information, finally, is a question of assembling scattered facts and interpreting them for others. Shaping data in this way is a skill that needs exercise. It is an act of education and, of course, an act of control.

The final positive outcome for information-rich individuals is that information flows to them as well as away from them. This ability to attract, create, and disseminate information can become an immense managerial asset, a self-perpetuating information network, and a means of creating the trust that the upward flow of candid information depends on.

Originally published in March–April 1989
Reprint 89203

Skilled Incompetence

CHRIS ARGYRIS

Executive Summary

MOST MANAGERS SEE CIVILITY as an asset. Many top executives pride themselves on their skill in avoiding conflict. The rationale is it's best not to upset others. So with the best of intentions, managers try not to hurt the feelings of others. What happens, though, is that this civilized asset turns into a real liability.

When managers neither speak candidly nor put important facts on the table—including suspicions about others' motivations—they don't make effective decisions. If suspicions fester, if candor is lost, communication suffers, and so does the company.

Skilled incompetence is a condition in which people are very good at doing things that have unhappy consequences, even though they seem like the right thing to do. "Skilled" because, like riding a bicycle or playing tennis, people do it without thinking. "Incompetence" because it creates results that aren't intended, like falling off a bike. To avoid the disastrous organizational consequences that this special kind of incompetence produces, it helps to understand and recognize how deeply ingrained one's incompetences can be and how to unlearn them. Argyris recommends a special application of the case method as a first step in recognizing and unlearning what's wrong.

THE ABILITY TO GET ALONG with others is always an asset, right? Wrong. By adeptly avoiding conflict with coworkers, some executives eventually wreak organizational havoc. And it's their very adeptness that's the problem. The explanation for this lies in what I call skilled incompetence, whereby managers use practiced routine behavior (skill) to produce what they do not intend (incompetence). We can see this happen when managers talk to each other in ways that are seemingly candid and straightforward. What we don't see so clearly is how managers' skills can become institutionalized and create disastrous side effects in their organizations. Consider this familiar situation:

The entrepreneur-CEO of a fast-growing medium-sized company brought together his bright, dedicated, hard-working top managers to devise a new strategic plan. The company had grown at about 45% per year, but fearing that it was heading into deep administrative trouble, the CEO had started to re-think his strategy. He decided he wanted to restructure his organization along more rational, less ad hoc, lines. As he saw it, the company was split between the sales-oriented people who

*sell off-the-shelf products and the people producing cus-
tom services who are oriented toward professionals. And
each group was suspicious of the other. He wanted the
whole group to decide what kind of company it was
going to run.*

*His immediate subordinates agreed that they must
develop a vision and make some strategic decisions.
They held several long meetings to do this. Although the
meetings were pleasant enough and no one seemed to be
making life difficult for anyone else, they concluded with
no agreements or decisions. "We end up compiling lists
of issues but not deciding," said one vice president.
Another added, "And it gets pretty discouraging when
this happens every time we meet." A third worried aloud,
"If you think we are discouraged, how do you think the
people below us feel who watch us repeatedly fail?"*

This is a group of executives who are at the top, who
respect each other, who are highly committed, and who
agree that developing a vision and strategy is critical.
Yet whenever they meet, they fail to create the vision
and the strategy they desire. What is going on here? Are
the managers really so incompetent? If so, why?

What Causes Incompetence

At first, the executives in the previous example believed
that they couldn't formulate and implement a good
strategic plan because they lacked sound financial data.
So they asked the financial vice president to reorganize
and reissue the data. Everyone agreed he did a superb
job.

But the financial executive reported to me, "Our
problem is *not* the absence of financial data. I can flood

them with data. We lack a vision of what kind of company we want to be and a strategy. Once we produce those, I can supply the necessary data." The other executives reluctantly agreed.

After several more meetings in which nothing got done, a second explanation emerged. It had to do with the personalities of the individuals and the way they work with each other. The CEO explained, "This is a group of lovable guys with very strong egos. They are competitive, bright, candid, and dedicated. But when we meet, we seem to go in circles; we are not prepared to give in a bit and make the necessary compromises."

Is this explanation valid? Should the top managers become less competitive? I'm not sure. Some management groups are not good at problem solving and decision making precisely because the participants have weak egos and are uncomfortable with competition.

If personality were really the problem, the cure would be psychotherapy. And it's simply not true that to be more effective, executives need years on the couch. Besides, pinpointing personality as the issue hides the real culprit.

THE CULPRIT IS SKILL

Let's begin by asking whether counterproductive behavior is also natural and routine. Does everyone seem to be acting sincerely? Do things go wrong even though the managers are not being destructively manipulative and political?

For the executive group, the answer to these questions is yes. Their motives were decent, and they were at their personal best. Their actions were spontaneous, automatic, and unrehearsed. They acted in milliseconds; they were skilled communicators.

How can skillful actions be counterproductive? When we're skillful we usually produce what we intend. So, in a sense, did the executives. In this case, the skilled behavior—the spontaneous and automatic responses—was meant to avoid upset and conflict at the meetings. The unintended by-products are what cause trouble. Because the executives don't say what they really mean or test the assumptions they really hold, their skills inhibit a resolution of the important intellectual issues embedded in developing the strategy. Thus the meetings end with only lists and no decisions.

This pattern of failure is not only typical for this group of managers. It happens to people in all kinds of organizations regardless of age, gender, educational background, wealth, or position in the hierarchy. Let me illustrate with another example that involves the entire organizational culture at the upper levels. Here we'll begin to see how people's tendency to avoid conflict, to duck the tough issues, becomes institutionalized and leads to a culture that can't tolerate straight talk.

Where the Skillful Thrive

The top management of a large, decentralized corporation was having difficulty finding out what some of its division presidents were up to. Time and time again the CEO would send memos to the presidents asking for information, and time and time again they'd send next to nothing in return. But other people at headquarters accepted this situation as normal. When asked why they got so little direct communication from their division heads, they'd respond, "That's the way we do things around here."

Here is an organization that isn't talking to itself. The patterns that managers set up among themselves have become institutionalized, and what were once characteristic personal exchanges have now become organizational defensive routines. Before I go on to describe what these routines look like, let's look at how this situation arose.

Built into decentralization is the age-old tug between autonomy and control: superiors want no surprises, subordinates want to be left alone. The subordinates push for autonomy; they assert that by leaving them alone, top management will show its trust from a distance. The superiors, on the other hand, try to keep control through information systems. The subordinates see the control devices as confirming their suspicions—their superiors don't trust them.

Many executives I have observed handle this tension by pretending that the tension is not there. They act as if everyone were in accord and trust that no one will point out disagreements and thereby rock the boat. At the same time, however, they do feel the tension and can't help but soft-pedal their talk. They send mixed messages. (See "Four Easy Steps to Chaos" at the end of this article.) The CEO in this example kept saying to his division presidents, "I mean it—you run the show down there." The division presidents, wanting to prove their mettle, believed him until an important issue came up. When it did the CEO, concerned about the situation and forgetting that he wanted his division chiefs to be innovative, would make phone calls and send memos seeking information.

Defensive Routines Emerge

One of the most powerful ways people deal with potential embarrassment is to create "organizational defensive routines." I define these as any action or policy designed to avoid surprise, embarrassment, or threat. But they also prevent learning and thereby prevent organizations from investigating or eliminating the underlying problems.

Defensive routines are systemic in that most people within the company adhere to them. People leave the organization and new ones arrive, yet the defensive routines remain intact.

To see the impact of the defensive routines and the range of their effects, let's return to the division heads who are directed by mixed messages. They feel a lack of trust and are suspicious of their boss's intentions but they must, nonetheless, find ways to live with the mixed messages. So they "explain" the messages to themselves and to their subordinates. These explanations often sound like this:

> "Corporate never *really* meant decentralization."

> "Corporate is willing to trust divisions when the going is smooth, but not when it's rough.

> "Corporate is more concerned about the stock market than about us."

Of course, the managers rarely test their hypotheses about corporate motives with top executives. If discussing mixed messages among themselves would be uncomfortable, then public testing of the validity of these explanations would be embarrassing.

But now the division heads are in a double bind. On the one hand, if they go along unquestioningly, they may lose their autonomy and their subordinates will see them as having little influence with corporate. On the other, if the division executives do not comply with orders from above, headquarters will think they are recalcitrant, and if noncompliance continues, disloyal.

Top management is in a similar predicament. It senses that division managers have suspicions about headquarters' motives and are covering them up. If headquarters makes its impression known, though, the division heads may get upset. If the top does not say anything, the division presidents could infer full agreement when there is none. Usually, in the name of keeping up good relations, the top covers up its predicament.

Soon, people in the divisions learn to live with their binds by generating further explanations. For example, they may eventually conclude that openness is a strategy that top management has devised intentionally to cover up its unwillingness to be influenced.

Since this conclusion is based on the assumption that people at the top are covering up, managers won't test it either. Since neither headquarters nor division executives discuss or resolve the attributions or the frustrations, both may eventually stop communicating regularly and openly. Once in place, the climate of mistrust makes it more likely that the issues become undiscussable.

Now both headquarters and division managers have attitudes, assumptions, and actions that create self-fulfilling and self-sealing processes that each sees the other as creating.

Under these conditions, it is not surprising to find that superiors and subordinates hold both good and bad feelings about each other. For example, they may say about each other: "They are bright and well intentioned but they have a narrow, parochial view"; or "They are interested in the company's financial health but they do not understand how they are harming earnings in the long run"; or "They are interested in people but they pay too little attention to the company's development."

My experience is that people cannot build on their appreciation of others without first overcoming their suspicions. But to overcome what they don't like, people must be able to discuss it. And this requirement violates the undiscussability rule embedded in the organizational defensive routines.

Is there any organization that does not have these hang-ups and problems? Some people suggest that getting back to basics will open lines of communication. But the proffered panacea does not go far enough; it does not deal with the underlying patterns. Problems won't be solved by simply correcting one isolated instance of poor performance.

When CEOs I have observed declared war against organizational barriers to candor and demanded that people get back to basics, most often they implemented the new ideas with the old skills. People changed whatever they could and learned to cover their asses even more skillfully. The freedom to question and to confront is crucial, but it is inadequate. To overcome skilled incompetence, people have to learn new skills—to ask the questions behind the questions.

Defensive routines exist. They are undiscussable. They proliferate and grow underground. And the social pollution is hard to identify until something occurs that blows things open. Often that something is a glaring error whose results cannot be hidden. The recent space shuttle disaster is an example. Only after the accident occurred were the mixed messages and defensive routines used during the decision to launch exposed. The disaster made it legitimate for outsiders to require insiders to discuss the undiscussable. (By the way, writing a tighter set of controls and requiring better communication won't solve the problem. Tighter controls will only enlarge the book of rules that William Rogers, chairman of the president's committee to investigate the Challenger disaster, acknowledged can be a cure worse than the illness. He pointed out that in his Navy years, when the players went by the book, things only got worse.)

Managers do not have the choice to ignore the organizational problems that these self-sealing loops create. They may be able to get away with it today, but they're creating a legacy for those who will come after them.

How to Become Unskilled

The top-management group I described at the beginning of this article decided to learn new skills by examining the defenses they created in their own meetings.

First, they arranged a two-day session away from the office for which they wrote a short case beforehand. The purpose of these cases was twofold. First, they allowed the executives to develop a collage of the problems they thought were critical. Not surprisingly, in this particular group at least half wrote on issues related to the product versus custom service conflict. Second, the cases provided a kind of window into the prevailing rules and routines the executives used. The form of the case was as follows:

1. In one paragraph describe a key organizational problem as you see it.

2. In attacking the problem, assume you could talk to whomever you wish. Describe, in a paragraph or so, the strategy you would use in this meeting.

3. Next, split your page into two columns. On the right-hand side, write how you would begin the meeting: what you would actually say. Then write what you believe the other(s) would say. Then write your response to their response. Continue writing this scenario for two or so double-spaced typewritten pages.

4. In the left-hand column write any of your ideas or feelings that you would not communicate for whatever reason.

The executives reported that they became engrossed in writing the cases. Some said that the very writing of their case was an eye-opener. Moreover, once the stories were distributed, the reactions were jocular. They enjoyed them: "Great, Joe does this all the time"; "Oh, there's a familiar one"; "All salespeople and no listeners"; "Oh my God, this is us."

What is the advantage of using the cases? Crafted and written by the executives themselves, they become vivid examples of skilled incompetence. They illustrate the skill with which each executive sought to avoid upsetting the other while trying to change the other's mind. The cases also illustrate their incompetence. By their own analysis, what they did upset the others, created suspicion, and made it less likely that their views would prevail.

The cases are also very important learning devices. During a meeting, it is difficult to slow down behavior produced in milliseconds, to reflect on it, and to change it. For one thing, it's hard to pay attention to interpersonal actions and to substantive issues at the same time.

Case of the Custom-Service Advocate

Thoughts and Feelings	Actual Conversation
He's not going to like this topic, but we have to discuss it. I doubt that he will take a company perspective, but I should be positive.	**I:** Hi Bill. I appreciate having the opportunity to talk with you about this custom service versus product problem. I'm sure that both of us want to resolve it in the best interests of the company.
	Bill: I'm always glad to talk about it, as you well know.
I better go slow. Let me ease in.	**I:** There are a rising number of situations where our clients are asking for custom service and rejecting the off-the-shelf products. I worry that your salespeople will play an increasingly peripheral role in the future.
	Bill: I don't understand. Tell me more.
Like hell you don't understand. I wish there was a way I could be more gentle.	**I:** Bill, I'm sure you are aware of the changes [I explain].
	Bill: No, I don't see it that way. My salespeople are the key to the future.
There he goes, thinking like a salesman and not like a corporate officer.	**I:** Well, let's explore that a bit.

A collage from several cases appears in the table "Case of the Custom-Service Advocate." It was written by executives who believed the company should place a greater emphasis on custom service.

The cases written by individuals who supported the product strategy did not differ much. They too were trying to persuade, sell, or cajole their fellow officers. Their left-hand columns were similar.

In analyzing their left-hand columns, the executives found that each side blamed the other for the difficulties, and they used the same reasons. For example, each side said:

"If you insist on your position, you'll harm the morale I've built."

"Don't hand me that line. You know what I'm talking about."

"Why don't you take off your blinders and wear a company hat?"

"It upsets me when I think of how they think."

"I'm really trying hard, but I'm beginning to feel this is hopeless."

These cases effectively illustrate the influence of skilled incompetence. In crafting the cases, the executives were trying not to upset the others and at the same time were trying to change their minds. This process requires skill. Yet the skill they used in the cases has the unintended side effects I talked about. In the cases, the others became upset and dug in their heels without changing their minds.

Here's a real problem. These executives and all the others I've studied to date can't prevent the counterproductive consequences until and unless they learn new skills. Nor will it work to bypass the skilled incompetence by focusing on the business problems, such as, in this case, developing a business strategy.

THE ANSWER IS UNLEARNING

The crucial step is for executives to begin to revise how they'd tackle their case. At their two-day seminar each manager selected an episode he wished to redesign so that it would not have the unhappy result it currently produced.

In rewriting their cases, the managers realized that they would have to slow things down. They could not produce a new conversation in the milliseconds in which they were accustomed to speak. This troubled them a bit because they were impatient to learn. They had to keep reminding themselves that learning new skills meant they had to slow down.

Each manager took a different manager's case and crafted a new conversation to help the writer of the episode. After five minutes or so, they showed their designs to the writer. In the process of discussing these new versions, the writer learned a lot about how to redesign his words. And, as they discovered the bugs in their suggestions and the way they made them, the designers also learned a lot.

The dialogues were constructive, cooperative, and helpful. Typical comments were:

"If you want to reach me, try it the way Joe just said."

"I realize your intentions are good, but those words push my button."

"I understand what you're trying to say, but it doesn't work for me. How about trying it this way?"

"I'm surprised at how much my new phrases contain the old messages. This will take time."

Practice is important. Most people require as much practice to overcome skilled incompetence as to play a not-so-decent game of tennis. But it doesn't need to happen all at once. Once managers are committed to change, the practice can occur in actual business meetings where executives set aside some time to reflect on their actions and to correct them.

But how does unlearning skilled incompetence lead to fewer organizational snafus? The first step is to make sure executives are aware of defensive routines that surround the organizational problems that they are trying to solve. One way to do this is to observe them in the making. For example, during a meeting of the top line and corporate staff officers in our large decentralized organization, the CEO asked why the line and staff were having problems working effectively. They identified at least four causes:

The organization's management philosophy and policies are inadequate.

Corporate staff roles overlap and lead to confusion.

Staff lacks clear-cut authority when dealing with line.

Staff has inadequate contact with top line officers.

The CEO appointed two task forces to come up with solutions. Several months later, the entire group met for a day and hammered out a solution that was acceptable to all.

This story has two features that I would highlight. First, the staff-line problems are typical. Second, the story has a happy ending. The organization got to the root of its problems.

But there is a question that must be answered in order to get at the organizational defensive routines. Why did all the managers—both upper and lower— adhere to, implement, and maintain inadequate policies and confusing roles in the first place?

Why open this can of worms if we have already solved the problem? Because defensive routines prevent executives from making honest decisions. Managers who are skilled communicators may also be good at covering up real problems. If we don't work hard at reducing defensive routines, they will thrive—ready to undermine this solution and cover up other conflicts.

Four Easy Steps to Chaos

HOW DOES A MANAGER SEND MIXED MESSAGES? It takes skill. Here are four rules:

1. Design a clearly ambiguous message. For example, "Be innovative and take risks, but be careful" is a message that says in effect, "Go, but go just so far" without specifying how far far is. The ambiguity and imprecision cover the speaker who can't know ahead of time what is too far.

   The receiver, on the other hand, clearly understands the ambiguity and imprecision. Moreover, he or she knows that a request for more precision would likely be interpreted as a sign of immaturity or inexperience. And the receivers may also need an out some day and may want to keep the message imprecise and ambiguous. Receivers don't want "far" defined any more clearly than the senders do.

2. Ignore any inconsistencies in the message. When people send mixed messages, they usually do it spontaneously and with no sign that the message is mixed. Indeed, if they did appear to hesitate, they would defeat their purpose of maintaining control. Even worse, they might appear weak.

3. Make the ambiguity and inconsistency in the message undiscussable. The whole point of sending a mixed message is to avoid dealing with a situation straight on. The sender does not want the message's mixedness exposed. An executive is not about to send a mixed message and then ask, "Do you find my message inconsistent and ambiguous?" The executive also renders the message undiscussable by the very natural way of sending it. To challenge the innocence of the sender is to imply that the sender is duplicitous—not a likely thing for a subordinate to do.

4. Make the undiscussability also undiscussable. One of the best ways to do this is to send the mixed message in a setting that is not conducive to open inquiry, such as a large meeting or a group where people of unequal organizational status are present. No one wants to launder linen in public. While they are sending mixed messages during a meeting, people rarely reflect on their actions or talk about how the organizational culture, including the meeting, makes discussing the undiscussable difficult.

Originally published in September–October 1986
Reprint 86501

The Hidden Messages
Managers Send

MICHAEL B. MCCASKEY

Executive Summary

IF A MANAGER IN AN ORGANIZATION talks about making an "end run," what is he saying? Is he seeing life in the organization as a game; is he seeing it as hazardous and maybe nominating himself for a hero role; or is he merely saying he's going all the way with a project, regardless. The truth is we don't know what he's saying. It is all too easy both to interpret the metaphors others use to fit our own meanings and to ignore the fact that metaphors have idiosyncratic meanings that should be listened to. The author describes three ways managers convey messages about themselves and the ways they see the world. He encourages the reader to see these ways—their metaphors, office settings, and body language and tones that accompany their speech—as means of communicating. Just as speech or mathematics, these are languages that can be learned. With skill in them, a manager can see or hear what is really going on when people talk, what hidden messages we are sending all the time. The author gives some hints on what to look and listen for in trying to understand others' but he warns against simplistic interpretations: all messages occur in context.

In THE COURSE OF AN ORDINARY DAY, the typical general manager spends an extraordinary amount of time meeting and talking with people. Part and parcel of a manager's communication are the imagery, the place, and the body movements that he or she uses. Images, setting, and body language are not just adjuncts to communication. They carry the messages; and indeed, in some cases, they *are* the messages. As such they are tremendously important to a manager. Yet managers often pay only haphazard attention to them or, worse, presume that they are not gifted in these areas. The truth is we all use these ways of communicating—whether we are aware of them or not. The gift is in knowing *what* is being communicated.

Like mathematics, French, and accounting, these are languages that can be learned. With intelligent practice, for example, a person can learn to read and to speak "place"—that is, to understand the symbolic, territorial, and behavior-influencing aspects of physical settings. Imagery, place, and body language rarely provide definitive information; but they do provide a manager with a way of knowing that is not available through other message channels. With skill in these languages, a manager can develop instincts and a good "feel" for a

problem that makes additional appreciation of its sub-
tleties possible.

If managers pay close attention to these features
embedded in their everyday work life, they will enhance
their awareness of communicating with others. In this
article, I will present some ideas for understanding and
practicing the languages and will indicate the right
direction the reader can take to learn more on his or her
own.

Managers' Words and Their Images

A senior vice president in a large New York bank is talking about the group he formerly worked with: "You hit
the bird cage and everyone is on a new perch. People are
always moving there. People move so fast, and they—
whew! I got out of there before it all came down."

The imagery is very graphic and tells a lot about this
man and the world he lives in. If you could listen to him
a little more, you would not be surprised to learn that he
does not have a traditional banking background. He sees
himself as an entrepreneur and feels that, while most of
them are attractively dressed and schooled, the other
executives in the bank don't have any fire in their guts.
En masse (he doesn't see them as individuals) "they" are
"birds," which suggests he thinks they are pretty, caged,
and—quite likely—fragile. One can sense the relief this
man felt when he moved to a part of the bank where he
could be active, be himself, be entrepreneurial.

When you pay close attention to the words other people use, you notice that most people draw characteristic
verbal pictures of themselves and the world around
them. The imagery and metaphors that a person most

frequently uses can be clues to understanding the world he or she inhabits. These vivid kernels of speech are drawn from the sports world, from literature, from religion, and from other fields of personal interest or background. The imagery shows what's valued, what's feared, and what the speaker's behavioral rules are.

Consider the following examples of imagery:

- "It's like a fugue, everyone has a different part to play."

- "What we do here is drop back five and punt."

- "I am prepared to wait until hell freezes over."

- "One more snide comment, and I would have exploded."

A recurring use of metaphors might suggest that a person sees life in the organization as a game or is fatalistic about outcomes. Metaphors can also reflect an optimistic, a pessimistic, or even a confused outlook. Think of your own metaphors. Can they be characterized as earthy, poetic, or violent? Taken in context, words in metaphor can be clues to how another is feeling, to what he or she views as important.

Another major point about the verbal environment of managers is that words are symbols, the meanings of which can vary greatly depending on who is using them. This point is troublesome, because it seems so obvious and at the same time contradicts an assumption we usually make in our everyday behavior. I have talked with managers who assume that words are entities and that communicating with another is essentially a process of logically ordering those entities. They direct all their efforts toward getting the words right and presenting a

logically structured train of thought in order to
persuade.

Much of the communication between two people,
however, implicitly involves sentiments and feelings.
These feelings are attached to the different experiences
that words connote for an individual. A typical conversation bumps along without either party paying close
attention to the different experiences and, therefore, the
different meanings that lie behind the words. We tend to
assume that we are all referring to the same thing when
we say "the boss," "a good report," "a viable alternative,"
and "a workable solution," but most likely we are not.

As you examine misunderstandings between two
managers, you will often find that what fouls the channels of communication is their mutual assumption that
they are using the same words to mean the same things.
A division vice president and general manager of a large
consumer products company was in the early stages of
trying to inculcate a team management style for his top
group of managers. At one meeting his marketing vice
president asked, "Who is driving the bus?"—implying
that no one was. This was a clear metaphor based on
familiar experience, probably made stronger by the
active connotation of "driving" and the echo of "bus" in
the word *business.* However, the seemingly clear question sparked off heated disagreement. The senior executive heard the marketing vice president saying he was
uncomfortable that there would not be one person in
charge. That was not at all what the division vice president had meant to convey by team management.

What makes communication problematic is that
people fail to recognize the personally distinctive ways
in which others use words. As Fritz Roethlisberger puts
it, "As a result, we fail to notice the differences, and we

read into our experiences similarities where differences exist."[1]

Keeping the differences in mind, try listening to conversations somewhat differently from usual. You might hear the following three features of the verbal environment:

- Does the person use concrete or abstract words? Different people are comfortable with different levels of abstraction. Some people use vivid, concrete expressions; others favor "-ism" and "-ion" words that describe states and conditions. A "concrete" listener might simply reject out of hand—and not bother listening to—someone who talks at a more abstract level, and vice versa.

- Does the person joke and kid a lot? Joking is one of the few ways some managers permit risky statements to be made. American managers especially allow each other greater leeway in delivering a hard truth if it is packaged as part of a joke.

- Does the person say "I" or "we" more often? With whom does the person identify? For what groups is he or she willing to say, "We need to . . ."? In addition, a speaker who uses the royal or editorial "we" to refer to an action that he or she has obviously performed alone (royalty and editors excepted) can sound pompous.

The emotional baggage that words carry shows up in other ways as well. In an aerospace company, two managers disagreed about the best way to approach top management for renewed funding of a promising research project. On the one hand, the group research director wanted to "provide a menu of options." He wanted not only to give some choices but also to specify the range without dramatically posing the stakes. By using the word *menu* he was saying, in effect, "After all, everybody has to eat something—the question is what."

On the other hand, the project manager wanted the company to "bite the bullet." He wanted to challenge top management to do it right (that is, to put big funding behind the project) or not to do it at all. Complete with overtones of the American Wild West and palpable dangers, his phrasing depicts a situation in which a big step—even though painful or risky—was necessary for the long-run health of the project. In this case, both managers are using words as emotional flags; their phrasing expresses very different sets of assumptions, values, and readings of company mission and philosophy.

Emotional flag waving can, however, be a real impediment to discussion. When a manager assigns a pejorative word (such as a "Casanova," "brown nose," "Commie") to another's point of view, he is labeling that person. In labeling, a person is using a word to stop or impede thinking; it represents a quick put-down. Without making an effort to understand the other's meanings, a person using a label often cuts off any thoughtful response. If the label is couched in a witty jibe, the offended party may find it particularly difficult to continue the discussion in terms of the issues. A manager who is a third party to such an exchange can play a valuable role in identifying the labeling for what it is and in restating the matter for continued discussion.

Another important aspect of the verbal environment of managers is questions. Why are they so important? Questions often contain assumptions that not only frame the problem in a certain way but also tend to force its resolution to conform to the implicit assumption.

In the example used earlier, one executive asked, "Who is driving the bus?" As I indicated, the question as phrased contains the assumption that *one* person should be doing the driving. But it also contains the assumption that anyone else is a back-seat driver, which is bad enough in a passenger car, but frightening in a busload of back-seat drivers. Both assumptions are antithetical to a team management concept. From the division vice president's point of view, that was the wrong question to be asking, and he was savvy enough to make the assumption in the question explicit and to challenge it.

But aren't there other aspects of questions that a manager needs to attend to? Well, yes. Questions are not always what they appear to be. Some, like the one I just posed, are really disguised statements. Gestalt psychologist Fritz Perls would sometimes refuse to answer questions that patients put to him. He thought of them as traps, inviting him to be the power figure. He wanted people to acknowledge their own power and to face up to the statements they needed to make without hiding behind them as questions. In addition, Roethlisberger has noted that some (perhaps many) questions are so silly they don't deserve to be answered.[2]

Yet in the United States, people feel obliged to answer a question, even though answering should depend on whether the question is a good one, whether it is posed at the right time, and whether a person wants to answer. You might find it revealing to pay attention to the questions you and others ask in conversations. See how many of the questions are really statements. A question is *not* as simple as it seems.

Finally, in considering how people reveal themselves through the words they use, look out for "either/or" thinking. Some people habitually frame discussions in these terms: something is either right or wrong; you are either with me or against me; a job is either good or bad.

Studies of the development of the mind have found that either/or thinking characterizes the early stages of a young adult's development. In time, most people discover that life is multidimensional and does not fit into two neat categories. Under stress, however, one can return to dichotomized thinking; it becomes time to "throw the crooks out" without investigating either whether they really are crooks or whether throwing crooks out is the most appropriate response. It is much easier to stereotype the opposition—and let thinking and efforts to understand end there—than it is to search for a more complex truth.

When you hear yourself or another manager discuss a situation in either/or terms, you might examine whether a two-value framework is, in that situation, posing false choices. There may be ways to synthetically create a new solution that incorporates something of both sides. The discussion then moves from thinking in either/or terms to thinking in both/and terms.

Words and imagery provide clues to the meanings and the important values, assumptions, and experiences that lie behind a person's choice of words. Next I examine how the place and character of a physical setting can influence communication between two people.

The Office and Place of Business

Depending on who they are and what kind of interactions they want with others, people use physical spaces in distinctive ways. Yet it often happens that both the receiver and the sender of messages about place are unaware of what is being communicated. A manager who becomes a little more thoughtful can better read what people are saying through their use of place. Managers can also examine their own physical settings to see if their arrangements influence behavior in ways that serve their ends.

The first thing to understand about place is that it represents territory. Animals mark off the range of their territory and defend it against intruders, and so does the human animal. Fences, doors, and boundary markers of all sorts separate what belongs to one person from what belongs to the rest of the world. Boundaries give security and privacy, protecting one from unwanted encroachments by others (at least boundaries make the statement that they are unwanted). For example, after a heavy snowfall in some Boston neighborhoods, people will claim as theirs the part of the street they have shovelled for parking. While the car is away, they will mark their claims with chairs or trash cans and strenuously object should anyone try to move in on "their spot."

For people to have a sense of "their own" and "home" seems quite important. Basketball teams like UCLA and Notre Dame are especially tough to beat when they have the home-court advantage. Home is familiar, predictable, and mine. The importance of having one's own territory shows up in a study of communal space in Coventry, England. Contrary to what one might expect, those families that had their own yards fraternized more than the families who shared a communal yard.

In analyzing this finding, one commentator suggests, "In suburbs and small towns, people are more likely to talk across their backyards if the property line is indicated by a fence. Because this boundary helps them maintain territoriality, it actually brings neighbors closer together."[3] This observation echoes Robert Frost's famous line, "Good fences make good neighbors."

The importance of place as territory shows up in the office as well. When a boss and a subordinate meet, whose office do they use? If the boss is sensitive to place as territory, the purpose of the meeting will decide the question. To conduct an adversary discussion, to emphasize hierarchy and authority, or to give directions, the boss should hold the meeting in his or her office. If, however, the boss wants to reach out to the subordinate—to have a conversation more on the other's terms—he or she might well consider traveling to the subordinate's office.

I know a manager who took the territoriality of office to heart. Just before beginning a tough negotiation session at another manager's office, he managed to sit in the other's big, ostentatious chair. He made light of his sitting in it by remarking on the feel of the chair as he swiveled from side to side. The second man was sufficiently discomfited by this unusual tactic that he lost the home-court advantage.

At the same time that place defines territoriality, other features of the setting also influence behavior, including the amount and type of interaction among people. Thomas Allen at MIT has studied communication patterns in R&D offices. He finds that beyond a distance of 25 or 30 yards personal interaction drops off markedly.[4] This suggests that a manager should physically locate together people in the organization who have the greatest need to talk to each other. If you are starting up a new team, locate core members close together, even if this means sacrificing status space for some members. When younger managers understand the dynamics of propinquity, they may try to locate their offices next to the boss's.

A manager can use the spaces in his or her office to influence the character of interactions there. For instance, many managers set up their offices with two different areas. In one, the manager talks across a desk to a person seated at the other side. Such an arrangement emphasizes the manager's authority and position. A subordinate is likely to feel that here the boss exercises a home-court advantage. In a second area, chairs are grouped around a coffee table or are placed at right angles to each other. Because this arrangement signals a willingness to downplay hierarchical differences, it encourages freer exchange and perhaps more sociable encounters.

Managers in a large financial services company I know are perfect examples of how people display instinctive reactions to physical settings. They have a marked preference for using one of four conference rooms, which are all alike except for the tables. Three of the rooms have rectangular tables that can be moved into squares or U-shapes; the fourth and most popular room has a round table. For reasons having to do with the culture and norms of this organization, the managers much prefer to work with each other around the round table.

Physical settings can be used in other ways to control interactions among people. A buyer for an electronics company housed in a building that lacked an elevator deliberately located his office on the third floor. A salesperson coming to the reception desk on the first floor would invariably be told that the buyer "could see you immediately." The salesperson would then trek the 40 steps to the buyer's office and, while still out of breath and somewhat disoriented, be greeted by the buyer.[5] In this case, physical setting was designed to control the interaction, beginning it on terms that put the salesperson at a disadvantage.

The impact these arrangements have on people is consistent with what cultural anthropologists have observed concerning people's sense of personal space. Edward T. Hall has studied how people in different cultures vary in what constitutes a comfortable distance for talking. His research shows that while the English and Germans stand farther apart than Americans when talking, the Arabs and Japanese stand closer together. Hall also identifies four basic distances for interaction: intimate space (touching to 18 inches); personal space (18 inches to 4 feet); social space (4 feet to 12 feet); and public space (12 feet and beyond).[6]

With chairs at right angles people can more easily move into each other's personal space. When a desk is placed between two people, the interaction shifts from a personal space to a social space. The content and nature of communication between two people change markedly when they move from one spatial zone to another. As a result of furniture arrangement, then, people often do become more distant—in both senses of the term.

The physical setting also influences behavior because it symbolizes the status of the occupants. Managers sense this, and one sometimes sees terrific battles fought over physical space in organizations as members vie for the visible manifestation of a more subtle and elusive phenomenon—power and influence. John Dean noticed this in his first days at the White House:

"As Bud and I went past the offices of White House staff members, I noticed furniture and files being moved. The White House, far more than any other government office, was in a state of perpetual internal flux. Offices were constantly exchanged and altered. . . .

"Everyone jockeyed for a position close to the President's ear, and even an unseasoned observer could sense minute changes in status. Success and failure could be seen in the size, decor, and location of offices. Anyone who moved to a smaller office was on the way down. If a carpenter or wallpaper hanger was busy in someone's office, this was a sure sign he was on the rise. Every day, workmen crawled over the White House complex like ants. Movers busied themselves with the continuous shuffling of furniture from one office to another as people moved in, up, down, or out. We learned to read office changes as an index of the internal bureaucratic power struggles."

By White House standards Dean's first office was shabby. When he complained, he was told it was only temporary, that Haldeman hadn't decided where to put him yet: "I did not have to be told what was happening. I was being tested and my performance would determine what I would get. I was at the bottom of the ladder, and instinctively, I began to climb."[7]

From the manager's point of view, control over personal furnishings enhances power and authority. Or, depending on how he uses his office, the manager can emphasize other values that he considers essential to the high performance of the company.

Ken Olsen and the other top managers at Digital Equipment Corporation have built one of the most successful minicomputer companies in the world. Their offices in an old mill are far from grand. Sometimes separated by plywood partitions, the offices are faithful to the simple, Spartan beginnings of the company. These arrangements send very clear messages to the managers and to visitors—hard work and what is functional are important at DEC. Some may disagree with the DEC managers' choices now that they are so successful, but, regardless, they reveal the range possible in using physical space to support and convey the essential values of the organization.

Although it's easier to see when visiting another organization, you might tour your own and look at the messages you send by your use of physical space. Try touring it as if it were another company. How much of the space (and information) is locked up? Are files, phones, and offices fastened shut? How carefully do differences in the size, location, and furnishings of offices mark status?

Look at the bulletin boards. If they are extremely neat and if notices must be initialed, employees will feel less free to scrawl their own notes or to put up cartoons. Is there a coffee urn or somewhere else that serves as a "watering hole," or are people isolated from one another by the office layout? An informed reading of place can reveal a lot about how tight a company is, how hierarchical, how rules conscious, whether individual expression is encouraged, and what the company values.

Most individuals set up their office spaces to encourage certain types of interaction and, consciously or not, to send messages about themselves. When I enter a person's place for the first time, I often look at how much he or she has personalized it with pictures of family, mentors, friends, or favorite places. How much does that person declare about himself? Who are the special people, what kinds of things does he enjoy having around?

When you first walk into an office or a home, notice the textures. If the person had a choice, did he use tactile fabrics, long-haired rugs, coverings that invite a vistor to run a hand over them? This person may be signaling a desire to "be in touch," to interact at a closer distance. Or are the surfaces clean, polished, and smooth? Does the owner seem to prefer orderliness, to keep interactions at more of a distance? You might look at your own spaces in the same way and try to read the messages that others might find there about you and your preferred styles of interacting.

Body Language and Paralinguistics

Like physical settings, body language and paralinguistics convey important messages that color, support, or contradict the words people use. They send nonverbal messages, although in the case of paralinguistics (which includes the tone of voice, pacing, and other extralinguistic features that surround talking), they can involve sounds.

A project director in a huge aerospace company called a meeting of higher management people who supported his research project. Consonant with the oft-expressed company policy of commercially exploiting advanced research work, he wanted them to fund development of a new product internally. Early in the meeting, as he began to outline the sizable costs involved, he sensed their disapproval from facial expressions and body postures. His intuition told him that if they were asked to make an explicit decision on the project, it would be negative. So he changed his line of argument and began stressing the possibilities for external rather than internal funding of the project. And he assiduously avoided asking for a funding decision at that time.

This type of nonverbal communication and adjustment occurs every day in business, but frequently it goes unnoticed. Messages that are key to a situation—but that participants feel cannot be publicly or verbally acknowledged—are sent through these channels. Because nonverbal messages are ambiguous and subtle, one can readily reinterpret or deny them. Paradoxically, such messages can be safer and truer precisely because they are not precise. In the aerospace company, both the project director and higher management had their own reasons for keeping the communication ambiguous.

Several books have appeared lately in the popular press that claim to remove the ambiguity from body language. They offer a single translation for many facial expressions and body postures. For example, arms crossed against the chest "means" that the listener has closed his mind to what the speaker is saying. This kind of simplistic interpretation is an unfortunate misuse of the scholarly research on nonverbal communication. No gesture has a single, unvarying meaning. The researchers have stressed that the meaning of any gesture depends on cultural norms, personal style, the physical setting, what has gone before, and what both parties anticipate for the future.

Even when the person and the context are fairly well known, one should be cautious in interpreting body language. Recently I was walking down a company hallway with a staff person of a large manufacturer. We passed and exchanged greetings with a man named Jim who was just coming from a meeting where he had learned of his new assigmment. His face was sagging, and his walk and carriage lacked their usual briskness.

Later at lunch we spent several minutes comparing our readings of Jim's nonverbal behavior, searching for alternative explanations, and wondering what each possibility might suggest for the department's future. Interpretations like this should be made cautiously and tentatively. We might find out, for example, that Jim was suffering from the flu—and that was the main source of his nonverbal behavior.

Keeping in mind that nonverbal languages are useful (because they are ambiguous) and the need for interpreting meanings within context, let us see how a manager could learn to read nonverbal languages with greater understanding. For many, the face is the most obvious conveyor of feelings—so obvious, in fact, that we have the expression, "It was written all over his face." Some research indicates that facial expression, along with tone of voice, accounts for more than 90% of the communication between two people. The dictionary meaning of words, then, accounts for only about 10% of the communication.[8]

The best way to improve one's reading of facial expressions is to watch soundless videotape or film of people's faces as they talk. Watch for raising or knitting of the eyebrows, widening of the pupils, flaring or wrinkling of the nose, tightening of the lips, baring or clenching of the teeth. To take one example, dilating pupils tend to mean that the listener is interested in what you are saying; contracting pupils suggest he or she does not like what you are saying.

But reading a facial expression is a complex process because a face often shows a mixture of several feelings at once, matching the mixture of feelings that the person may be experiencing inside.

Eye-to-eye contact is one of the most direct and powerful ways people communicate nonverbally. In U.S. culture, the social rules suggest that in most situations eye contact for a short period is appropriate. Prolonged eye contact is usually taken to be either threatening or, in another context, a sign of romantic interest. Most managers are aware that they look directly at individual members of an audience to enhance the impact of their presentation. Some, however, are not aware of how important eye contact is when they are listening. A good listener must be physically active to show good attention.

Among whites in the United States, the general rule is that the *speaker* in a conversation should find a way to break eye contact and look away. The *listener* shows attention by spending relatively more time looking at the speaker. Because it makes it harder for the speaker to continue, communication difficulties arise if the listener looks away too often. Knowing the impact looking away has can help a manager signal how much longer he or she wishes the other to continue speaking.

For example, in situations where the boss wishes to hear out the subordinate, he or she should be careful to provide the encouragement of eye attention, head nodding, and occasional "uh huhs" as the other is speaking. Even without saying words, a manager is sending nonverbal messages about the depth of his or her understanding and the degree of empathy.

The unspoken norms about patterns of eye contact do differ among racial groups. For blacks or Chicanos looking away does not necessarily mean the same lack of attention that it might mean among white speakers. A young white businessman learned this lesson in his first year of managing a subsidiary in a predominantly Chicano community. He was reprimanding a clerk named Carlos for a repeated error in record keeping. As he tried to discuss the matter, Carlos kept averting his eyes. The manager became angry and said, "Look at me when I'm talking to you." The young stock boy tried to establish eye contact but could not maintain it for long.

To the manager, this signaled disrespect and possibly defiance. For the stock boy (following his own cultural norms), it would have been a sign of disrespect to maintain eye contact with a boss who was reprimanding him. It was only after Carlos became extremely discomfited that the manager realized that Carlos's behavior was not meant to communicate disrespect. Thus patterns of nonverbal communication are highly variable among different cultures and groups, and one should be cautious in generalizing too broadly. Assuming that everyone follows the same rules can lead to misinterpretations.

The paralinguistic features of speech offer another powerful means of tuning in to another's feelings. How is something said? Paralanguage includes tone and quality of voice, pitch, pacing of speech, and sounds such as sighs or grunts. Managers can treat paralanguage as the music of communication—to observe how a person's voice tightens or catches at difficult passages or rushes and soars at moments of high emotion. Surprisingly, one can often hear the voice of another better without accompanying visual information. Because verbal messages can be distracting (an overload) or contradictory to the music of paralanguage, we do not attend as closely as we might to this valuable data source in face-to-face meetings.

Managers should notice pauses and silences as well as the pacing of speech. Silences can have a whole range of meanings. At one extreme, people use them as a weapon or tactic to close a sale or to seek agreement— waiting until the other is discomfited enough to make some concession toward their positions. Used another way, a pause in the conversation can be a valuable gift that allows the other person time to consider carefully

his or her thoughts and feelings. The nonverbal behavior
a person uses during the silence can help convey
whether he or she intends one or the other effect.

One special type of pause is the *filled pause,* in which
the speaker uses a sound such as "uhhh" to fill the
spaces between words. Sociologist Erving Goffman notes
that filled pauses are used to "provide continuity, showing that the speaker is still in the business of completing
a reply even though he cannot immediately muster up
the right words to effect this."[9] A filled pause is a signal
that preserves the speaker's right to talk since it says, in
effect, "Don't interrupt. I'm still talking."

The hidden messages of body language and paralanguage do not have to be the same as the verbal ones;
and, in fact, a one-to-one correspondence is unlikely.
But in situations where full and open communication is
the aim, the nonverbal messages should add to the verbal ones in ways that are reasonable and trustworthy.
When a person is communicating well, the body language moves in concert with the words. Smaller movements such as dropping the head, the hands, or the eye's
gaze mark a pause, emphasize a point, or express some
doubt or irony in one's speech. To mark larger transi-
tions in thought, the speaker will change his body position altogether.[10] Nonverbal behavior, then, serves as
punctuation for the verbal messages being sent.

In moments of great rapport, a remarkable pattern of
nonverbal communication can develop. Two people will
mirror each other's movements—dropping a hand, shifting their body at *exactly* the same time.[11] This happens
so quickly that without videotape or film replay one is
unlikely to notice the mirroring. But managers can learn
to watch for disruptions in this mirroring because they
are dramatically obvious when they occur. In the midst

of talking, when a person feels that the other has violated his expectations or values, he or she will often signal distress. If norms or status differences make it unwise to express disagreement or doubt verbally, then the message will be conveyed through nonverbal "stumbles."

Instead of smooth mirroring, there will be a burst of movement, almost as if both are losing balance. Arms and legs may be thrust out and the whole body posture changed in order to regain balance.[12] Stumbles signal the need to renegotiate what's being discussed. The renegotiation occurs very rapidly and subtly and often through nonverbal channels. Managers who are aware of stumbles and what they mean have an option open to them that unaware managers do not. They can decide whether a given situation could be more effectively dealt with by verbally discussing it.

As with other languages, a manager can increase skill in sending nonverbal messages through intelligent practice. One helpful approach is to isolate and study one channel at a time. Because more information comes through several channels than one person can handle in a face-to-face encounter, for purposes of learning a person should try to latch on to one set of details at a time. Isolating a channel allows one to appreciate more fully the complexity and richness of each channel.

For example, one way managers can increase their listening skills and sharpen their appreciation of body language is by replaying videotapes of their own and others' behavior or by watching television without the sound. Listening to audiotapes and hearing the music of paralanguage is also instructive.

The nonverbal channels often convey messages too sensitive for explicit verbal communication. Since the messages are subtle, ambiguous, and often tentative, they must be read with caution in order to realize their potential richness. These hidden messages reinforce or contradict what is proclaimed verbally and thus can aid an aware manager in making sense of a situation.

Reading the Messages

One of the ways a manager can develop skill in all three languages is to work in a small group. It's often instructive for managers to try out proposed solutions to a managerial problem by playing roles while others watch. The observers will often be surprised at how quickly they can tell if one of the role players is feeling under attack or is trying to mislead the other. Even though a role player thinks he is hiding his discomfort or impatience, observers read the hidden messages quite clearly, although the role players themselves may not be aware of them.

Two lessons emerge. First, for those who are uncomfortable with the idea that they may be giving themselves away, it is very difficult to censor these messages. They "leak out" one way or another. Trying to censor them only increases the confusion of signals and diverts energy that could better be directed toward understanding what is going on. Second, body language, paralinguistics, and imagery are always part of an interaction. The messages are there to be read. With practice a manager can increase skill in reading and sending these messages, even to the point of being able to attend to them while in the middle of a specific situation.

In summary, none of these three languages alone gives a clear-cut message about the people using them. But cumulatively they can form the basis for impressions and hunches to be checked out through further inquiry. Our physical settings, like the clothes we wear, the words we utter, and the gestures we make, communicate to others about us and influence others with regard to us. Whether we are aware of it or not, our interactions with people will be affected by what they learn about us through our imagery, settings, and body language—and by what we learn about them through theirs.

Notes

1. Fritz J. Roethlisberger, *Management and Morale* (Cambridge, Mass.: Harvard University Press, 1941), p. 98.

2. Roethlisberger, *Management and Morale*, p. 100.

3. David Dempsey, "Man's Hidden Environment," *Playboy*, May 1972, p. 108.

4. Thomas J. Allen, "Communication Networks in R&D Laboratories," *R&D Management*, Vol. 1, 1970, p. 14.

5. Luise Cahill Dittrich, "The Psychology of Place," ICCH 9-476-086, distributed by the Intercollegiate Case Clearing House, Soldiers Field, Boston, Mass. 02163.

6. Edward T. Hall, *The Hidden Dimension* (New York: Doubleday, 1966).

7. John W. Dean III, *Blind Ambition* (New York: Simon & Schuster, 1976), p. 29.

8. Albert Mehrabian, "Communication Without Words," *Psychology Today*, September 1968, p. 52.

9. Erving Goffman, *Frame Analysis: An Essay on the Organization of Experience* (New York: Harper & Row, 1974), p. 543.

10. W.S. Condon and W.D. Ogston, "A Segmentation of Behavior," *Journal of Psychiatric Research*, Vol. 5, 1967, p. 221; and Albert E. Scheflen, *How Behavior Means* (Garden City, N.Y.: Doubleday, 1974).

11. Ray L. Birdwhitsell, *Kinesics and Context* (Philadelphia: University of Pennsylvania Press, 1970).

12. Frederick Erickson, "Gatekeeping and the Melting Pot: Interaction in Counselling Encounters," *Harvard Educational Review*, Vol. 45, February 1975, p. 44.

Originally published in November–December 1979
Reprint 79609

The author would like to thank Luise Cahill Dittrich for her help on an earlier version of this article that appeared in Anthony G. Athos and John J. Gabarro, Interpersonal Behavior: Communication and Understanding in Relationships *(Englewood Cliffs, N.J.: Prentice-Hall, 1978).*

Reaching and Changing Frontline Employees

T.J. LARKIN AND SANDAR LARKIN

Executive Summary

PLANNING A MAJOR CHANGE in your organization?
If so, chances are your have arranged a huge rally,
rousing speeches, videos, and special editions of the
company paper. Stop. This sort of communication is not
working. If you want people to change they way they
do their jobs, you must change the way you communicate with them.

Drawing on their own research and the research of
other communication experts from the past two decades,
the authors argue that senior managers—and most communication consultants—have refused to hear what frontline workers have been trying to tell them: When you
need to communicate a major change, stop communicating values, communicate face-to-face, and spend
most of your time, money, and effort on frontline
supervisors.

Frontline employees don't want to find out about a change by watching a video. Nor do they want to read about it in a company publication, which they know is untrustworthy and usually incomprehensible. Large meetings won't do the trick, either. Change may be acceptable to employees, but empty slogans won't be.

Despite research showing that frontline employees prefer to receive information from their supervisor—the person to whom they are closest—companies continue to depend on charismatic executives to inspire the troops. Why doesn't this work? Because frontline supervisors are the real opinion leaders in any company. Senior managers must discuss a change face-to-face with supervisors, who will pass information along to their subordinates. Communication between frontline supervisors and employees counts the most toward changed behavior where it matters the most: at the front line.

MOST ADVICE GIVEN TO EXECUTIVES about communicating change is wrong. The advice usually boils down to *more:* more values, missions, and vision; more videos, publications, and meetings; more executive road shows. This communication is not working. Why would anyone want more of it?

More of what executives already do will not solve their communication problems. Practical experience and decades of research suggest a new approach. In 1993, Wyatt Company (now Watson Wyatt Worldwide) investigated 531 U.S. organizations undergoing major restructuring. Wyatt asked the CEOs, If you could go back and change one thing, what would it be? The most

frequent answer: The way I communicated with my
employees. The next time you communicate major
change to your frontline employees, do it differently.
Communicate only facts; stop communicating values.
Communicate face-to-face; do not rely on videos, publications, or large meetings. And target frontline super-
sors; do not let executives introduce the change to frontline employees.

Before going any further, let's clarify two points. First,
our advice concerns the communication of the sort of
change that most companies face every five to ten years.
We are talking about change that is necessary because
the company's survival may be at stake, not about everyday operational changes. Second, our advice is about
reaching and changing frontline employees in large
companies. Frontline employees such as bank tellers,
truck drivers, processors of insurance forms, airline
counter staff, welders, and telephone installers are the
people making the product or delivering the service. If
you want these people to change the way they do their
jobs, then you must change the way you communicate
with them.

Stop Communicating Values

The urge to wrap a change in a value is irresistible. But
the urge to communicate your values is proof positive
that you are not acting on them. The only effective way
to communicate a value is to act in accordance with it
and give others the incentive to do the same. If you value
customer service, for instance, then recruitment, performance appraisals, promotions, and bonuses should be
based on customer service performance. Creating objec-

tive measures for such performance will demonstrate your values much more clearly than your words ever can.

Stopping the value talk is itself a radical change, especially considering that, according to the Wyatt study, 68% of large companies consider missions and values to be their number one communication priority. We appeal to your intuition and common sense. Imagine meeting a business contact for the first time. This person hands you a card and says, "I want you to know my values. They are written here: I promise not to lie, cheat, or steal during any business transaction." Does that put you at ease? No—it makes you suspicious, and it does so because people reveal their values through their actions, not through their words. Talking about values signals that fraud is near.

> *If you break a rule that values are best communicated through actions, not through words, employees will punish you.*

What is true for people is true for organizations. In 1992, the Jensen Group, a change-management communication firm in Morristown, New Jersey, researched 23 large U.S. companies, including American Express, AT&T, Chemical Bank, IBM, Johnson & Johnson, Mobil, Texaco, and Warner-Lambert. Seventy percent of the companies hadrevised their corporate missions during recent restructuring; only 9% felt that revising their missions helped them achieve the objectives of the restructuring.

If you break the rule that values are best communicated through actions, employees will punish you. We have watched employees turn the slogans Quality in Everything We Make into Quality Is Everything We

Fake; Beliefs We Share into [Expletive] We Share; and Working with Pride into Working for [Expletive]. You might ask, Should we abandon our mission campaign just because of smart-aleck remarks from a handful of cynics? The question denies the reality. The frontline workforce is not sprinkled with a handful of cynics; it is cynical through and through. According to a study by Philip Mirvis and Donald Kanter published in the autumn 1989 issue of the *National Productivity Review,* 43% of employees believe that management cheats and lies. In their research, Mirvis and Kanter found that the frontline workforce is the most cynical group of all.

The latest wave of downsizings has made this bad situation worse. A 1994 study by the Council of Communication Management shows that 64% of employees believe that management is often lying. As reported in the *Wall Street Journal* (November 2, 1992), two-thirds of senior personnel managers surveyed by Right Associates, a human-resources consulting firm based in Philadelphia, said that employees trust management less after a restructuring. Face it: Employees will infer what you value from your behavior. They will adopt your values only if they are convinced that those values will enable them to attain their personal goals. Propaganda won't help.

In fact, it could hurt. At a large manufacturing company undergoing major change, thousands of employees watched as senior managers unveiled a new mission. Thousands more witnessed the unveiling by satellite. The slogan Trust, Teamwork, and Tomorrow was on a huge banner behind the speaker's platform. As employees left the presentation, they received pens, caps, and coffee mugs inscribed with the three Ts. When they returned to work, however, they found a letter to employees from the union posted on every bulletin board. This well-documented letter accused the company of hiring private investigators to watch employees suspected of stealing, using drugs, and making fraudulent disability claims. Investigators watched employees both during and after work, the letter claimed, and watched some employees even during the Trust, Teamwork, and Tomorrow launch.

Executives scrambled to rescue the new mission. Public relations consultants were called in to "explain to employees that hiring private investigators to watch them does not necessarily imply a lack of trust." The tragedy in the Trust, Teamwork, and Tomorrow example is not the embarrassment the executives felt but the damage done to the worthwhile changes wrapped in the value campaign. The changes themselves were acceptable to most employees. The empty words were not.

The solution is to communicate the facts—only the facts. Members of senior-management change teams must articulate in the fewest words possible what they plan to do. They must set those facts down on paper. This brief summary will become a change booklet that will guide face-to-face communication between senior managers and supervisors, and between supervisors and frontline employees.

The change booklets shown in the exhibit "Change Booklets: No Slogans, No Threats, No Pep Talks" were given to frontline supervisors by senior managers in face-to-face briefings. Both examples come from companies with which we have worked. The first change booklet was used by a bank that was creating regional business banking centers and moving its larger customers from neighborhood branches to the regional centers. The second example is from a manufacturing company that was preparing to lay off more than 2,000 employees.

These booklets are barely readable, but they are not meant to be read. They are meant to be explained and discussed. Notice what these examples do not have: punctuation, sentences, slogans, threats, pep talks. They contain nothing but facts.

Change Booklets: No Slogans, No Threats, No Pep Talks

Business Banking Centers

large business customers taken from branches

> moved to business banking centers

large = loans over $250,000 and/or balances over $250,000

handovers begin early May finished by September

business customers may remain in their branches

> customer must call business banking manager

> business banking manager must release customer

> bank wants to move as many as possible to the new centers

branches refer new customers to business banking centers

> 25% of loan or deposit credited back to branch's books

business banking centers have no cash

> transactions needing cash must go through a branch

Employee Reductions

2,300 employees will leave

begin November 4
> all leave by January 20

estimate only $\left[\begin{array}{l} \text{200 early retirement} \\ \text{1,100 voluntary} \\ \text{1,000 involuntary} \end{array}\right.$

if fewer go voluntarily
> more go involuntarily
> 2,300 is fixed

who selects involuntaries?
> crew supervisor (one or more)*
> shift superintendent
> human resources manager

*crew supervisor involved if supervised the employee for one year or more since 1990

Not communicating to employees during major organizational change is the worst mistake a company can make. Consider the conclusions from three important studies on communication during mergers and acquisitions: In periods of high stress and uncertainty, people fill communication voids with rumors; rumors end up attributing the worst possible motives to those in control; and communication lowers employees' stress and anxiety even when the news is bad. In other words, uncertainty is more painful than bad news.[1]

But, you might say, our change is too complicated to communicate in a matter-of-fact style. Then simplify the change. In large organizations, the limits of what you can communicate as facts are also the limits of what you can do. The prescriptions are simple: Cut out every unnecessary word. Avoid mission statements and management proclamations. Tell employees, straight up, exactly what you plan to do.

Communicate Face-to-Face

The best way to communicate a major change to the frontline workforce is face-to-face. Do not use videos or video hookups, do not introduce the change in a company publication, and do not hold large meetings with frontline employees.

VIDEOS

Over the past 15 years, video has been the fastest-growing medium for communicating with employees. This growth defies the fact that employees don't really want to watch videos. In the United States, video ranks eleventh out of 14 communication methods, according to studies conducted jointly by the International Association of Business Communicators and Towers, Perrin, Forster & Crosby (now Towers Perrin) in 1980, 1982, and 1984, and by TPF&C in 1990. According to a 1989 survey by the Industrial Society, a London-based training organization, British employees rated video thirteenth out of 16 ways to receive information. Sixty percent of large British companies have used videos to communicate major change, according to a 1993 study by the Institute of Management, a British trade association, yet 75% of those companies believe that the videos are ineffective. Our own survey of communication studies from the past 20 years suggests that across Canada, Australia, the United States, and Great Britain, employees prefer face-to-face communication to video at a rate of two to one.

Skip the research; use your intuition. A U.S. pizza chain needs to communicate a major change to employees and chooses to do so by distributing a video. What will happen? Will the teenage pizza cooks don their hats and hair nets, pull up chairs within inches of the TV, fold their hands, and watch the executive with utter seriousness? Or will they laugh, mimic the talking head, crack jokes, and throw bits of pepperoni at the screen? We suggest that the only place where the first scene actually occurs is in the minds of senior executives and that the image was probably planted there by communication consultants.

A threat to genuine communication even greater than the videocassette is on the horizon: digital video compression. This new technology reduces the cost of a satellite video channel from about $150,000 per month to only $15,000 per month. The enhanced quality of the image and the lowered cost will enable corporate executives to transmit their speeches live and then take questions through two-way hookups. The danger of this technology is that senior executives will use it. In front of the bright lights and rolling cameras, executives will reach into their bag of slogans and pull out the fluff: "delighting our customers," "becoming the best in the world," "working together as a family." They will then open the floor to an unrehearsed, unscripted flow of questions from the front line. In this situation, expect questions and comments to fall into three categories.

- The ridiculously specific question: "Our supplier packages salt in 40-pound sacks. That's too heavy. Can you possibly do something about that?" There's only one response to such questions: "I'll have to speak with your local manager and get back to you on that one."

- The goody-two-shoes comment: "Sounds like one heck of a challenge, but you can count on me." This remark appears innocent, but it isn't. The communication department will spend the next two weeks trying to convince everyone that it was not a setup.

- The I-hate-management diatribe: This is a short speech delivered by a particularly bitter employee whose anger is surpassed only by his or her rhetorical skill. The speech goes something like this: "People used to be proud to work for this company. But no longer. We gave you our trust and you shafted us. Everyone knows that morale in this place is in the dirt. All this company does is use people and then throw them away. How can you look at yourself in the mirror? After the way you have treated people, you should be ashamed." Meanwhile, 99% of the employees in the company lower their heads and mumble, "What a disaster." And the disaster they're referring to is not the hateful diatribe but the fact that management gave the floor to such an extreme individual.

Even before the first management platitude, even before the irrelevant, incredulous, or incendiary comments from employees, a terrible mistake has been made. A video presentation necessarily requires an audience. That is its inescapable flaw. When frontline employees are anticipating a major change, when they are becoming increasingly tense and worried, when their blood is beginning to run hot, the last thing you should do is gather them into a large group. In his 1896 book, *The Crowd*, French sociologist Gustave Le Bon described the "intensification of the emotions" and the "inhibition of the intellect" when individuals form a crowd. Think about that the next time you are practicing in front of the TelePrompTer before the big announcement.

PUBLICATIONS

Unlike a video, the company publication does not require the formation of a crowd. But it still has two major flaws in the eyes of frontline employees: It is untrustworthy and usually incomprehensible.

In the midst of major change in the early 1990s, Whirlpool asked its employees to evaluate the company publication, *Vision*. As reported in an article by Peter Moore in the March 1994 issue of *Communication World*, only 20% thought that the publication was "valuable and believable." The Whirlpool employees were probably being generous. A 1992 study by Mercer Management Consulting of 200 employee communication managers showed that 70% referred to their publications as "attempts at the truth," and less than 15% said that the publications reflected the entire truth.

The corporate publication process guarantees that a proposed organizational change will be neither believed nor understood. Think about it: An editor interviews the relevant managers and writes a story about the change. The story is then circulated to a dozen or so senior executives for comment. Each executive calls the editor and makes some vague suggestions for improving the piece. When the editor begins the final version, the audience is no longer the frontline workforce but the senior executives, each of whom will look for evidence of his or her influence in the final piece. The end product is an incredibly skillful, elaborately woven compromise— innocuous and unintelligible.

Many companies put up additional barriers to effective print communication. As Stephen Anderson reports in an article in the April 1994 issue of *Communication World*, GM/Saturn requires that all publications for employees be produced jointly by GM/Saturn management and the United Auto Workers. Another layer of overseers, interpreters, and censors is added, and more people in power must be appeased.

Think about what GM/Saturn has done, especially in light of GM's own research showing that only 8% of its employees prefer the union to the company itself as a source of information. This mistrust of unions is not limited to the UAW. According to Dennis Taylor's research on heavily unionized Australian companies published by the Australian Government Publishing Service in 1982, only 45% of employees believed that their union was usually or always telling the truth, whereas 96% said that their supervisors were usually or always telling the truth. GM/Saturn is undoubtedly trying to improve communication but is only adding another entity to be distrusted.

Again, use your common sense. On a day when your company's newspaper is delivered, visit the front line. Do employees dash into the supervisor's office, tear off the binding string, and hastily turn pages searching for articles on an upcoming change? No. These people are not fools. They know that the information in every article has been screened, qualified, pruned, softened, toned down, and hyped up.

Videos and publications can be useful tools, but not for introducing major change to frontline employees. Videos, for example, can convey technical information that is immediately applicable. Federal Express broadcasts videos on the best techniques for wrapping and shipping fragile packages. The U.S. Postal Service makes videos that show counter staff how to figure prices when rates change.

The company publication has two flaws in the eyes of frontline employees: It is untrustworthy and usually incomprehensible.

Videos are also useful when employees demand information that is not immediately relevant to them. For example, after the disastrous chemical leak in Bhopal, India, Union Carbide employees all over the world wanted to know how the tragedy happened and what the company was doing about it. Union Carbide's communication department went from making 4 videos per year to making 45. Such videos make good sense.

Similarly, publications can be valuable. At their best,

publications can guide informal face-to-face discussions. That is what the change booklets described earlier are meant to do. But print alone is not enough.

Many managers think that huge meetings will do the trick. They are wrong.

When a change requires frontline employees to do their jobs differently, that information must be delivered face-to-face, first in discussions between senior managers associated with the change and frontline supervisors, and then in discussions between the supervisors and their frontline subordinates.

MEETINGS

Many managers realize that communication should be face-to-face but think that huge meetings will do the trick. This is wrong. Face-to-face communication does not and should not mean large meetings when one has to communicate with frontline employees.

Stop for a moment. Let's ask the experts the best way to communicate with frontline employees. Who are the experts? Not big-name consultants. The experts are the frontline supervisors, the people who communicate with frontline employees daily. Researchers rarely ask those supervisors how they like to communicate. One of the few with the wisdom to do so is Janice A. Klein. Her study "Why Supervisors Resist Employee Involvement" (*Harvard Business Review* September–October 1984) shows that 85% of supervisors avoid meetings and prefer one-on-one communication.

Why? Supervisors know that any meeting with shop-floor workers can degenerate into a grievance session. Supervisors find that, as individuals, workers are reasonable and cooperative. In groups, however, a different mind-set prevails. What supervisor believes that it is a good idea to ask shop-floor employees to rally *publicly* behind a management initiative? Supervisors know that any employee who stands up in support of corporate-led changes will be branded a company stooge.

Communication professionals are wedded to the big bang theory of communication. "Of course there was communication," they say. "Weren't you at the Big Event?" In the belief that big events will generate excitement and demonstrate an organization's commitment, the professional communicators busy themselves in preparation. They arrange meeting times, reserve rooms, schedule temps to cover for employees at the meeting, prepare stacks of overhead transparencies, and book supervisors into the inevitable training course in communication skills.

The CEO of a large U.S. company enjoys telling this story: Her driver, cheerful as ever, picks her up at home and drives her to the office. Along the way, the CEO silently confronts her fear that layoffs may become necessary. Arriving at the office, she calls a meeting of the senior team and expresses her worry behind closed doors. Without better performance, she tells them, the company may have to lay people off. She leaves the meeting, takes the elevator to the basement garage, and steps into her car. The driver, with tears in his eyes, turns and asks, "How long have I got?"

Yes, rumors are usually inaccurate. But understand this about rumors: The transmission method is perfect.

The story exaggerates only slightly the astonishing speed with which rumors spread in large companies. But how? Who schedules the rumor meetings? Without temps and overtime, how do employees find time to pass on the rumor? Who prints the rumors onto overhead transparencies? And where are the trainers providing supervisors with refresher courses in rumor-communication skills?

The truth is there, but we refuse to see it. Corporate videos, publications, and meetings don't move information through companies; they inhibit it. The most effective way to communicate is informally, face-to-face, one-on-one. The problem with rumors is their inaccuracy. That is why face-to-face communication must be grounded in fact and in print. But understand this about rumors: The transmission method is perfect.

Target Frontline Supervisors

The first words employees hear about any change usually come from a corporate source: a senior manager, company newspaper, or video. Considering the front line's overwhelming mistrust of and hostility toward the corporate center, that practice is strange. No matter what the change—merger, restructuring, downsizing, reengineering, the introduction of new technology, or a customer service campaign—the first words frontline employees hear about a change should come from the person to whom they are closest: their supervisor.

Perhaps the employees in your company do not have negative feelings about senior managers. Having doubts? Try asking. In the midst of major changes during the early 1990s, many companies asked their employees what they thought of senior management. Employees at Colgate-Palmolive described their senior management team as lacking leadership, having no direction, not working well together, and being out of touch with cus-

tomers. Royal Bank of Scotland employees said that
senior managers were authoritarian and failed to treat
staff well, demanded more than they gave, and refused
to listen. British Telecom employees said that they had
little confidence in senior management and that the latest changes were bad for themselves personally, bad for
BT employees in general, and bad for BT as a company.
Employees at Whirlpool simply said, We didn't trust you
before and we don't trust you now. The relationship
between Rank Xerox senior managers and employees
was described as disastrous.[2]

Those companies need not feel embarrassed. The
trend of increasingly negative feelings toward senior
management transcends any individual company or
country. The companies men-
tioned above have simply been
brave enough to talk about it.
The people who should feel
embarrassed are the communication consultants who continue to recommend launch-
ing change from the top

*Research respected
since the 1940s
suggests that frontline
supervisors are
critical to the success
of any change effort.*

despite such findings. As the time for announcing a
major change comes closer, consultants line up outside
the offices of senior managers and spout the same
advice: "You've got to be more visible"; "You've got to be
seen as driving this change"; "Employees need to know
you've not fled to the bunker." This strategy may help
senior managers engage middle managers, but it won't
help them win over the front line. In fact, visibly associ-
ating senior executives with the change often increases
resistance among frontline employees.

Employees have been telling us for years that they
would rather receive information from their immediate

supervisors than from senior managers. We've simply refused to listen. The studies conducted jointly by the International Association of Business Communicators and Towers, Perrin, Forster & Crosby in 1980, 1982, and 1984, and by TPF&C in 1990 all reached the same conclusion: U.S. and Canadian employees prefer their immediate supervisors as sources of information. The Industrial Society found that British employees have the same preference. According to a 1993 study by International Survey Research, an organization based in Chicago that conducts employee-opinion surveys, the supervisor is the preferred information source for workers throughout Europe. Research that companies have conducted internally over the last two decades shows the same result: Ameritech, AT&T, Cadbury Schweppes, Exxon Chemical, GE, General Tire, GM, Hewlett-Packard, and Santa Fe all found that the immediate supervisor is the preferred source of information. Rarely does research speak in such a consistent voice. How should you respond to these findings? Spend 80% of your communication time, money, and effort on supervisors.

That is a radical recommendation. The traditional approach is to launch change from the top and hope that communication about the change will open like a parachute, blanketing everyone evenly. But frontline supervisors—not senior managers—are the opinion leaders in your organization. Because frontline supervisors greatly influence the attitudes and behaviors of others, they are critical to the success of any change effort. That realization, so radical to communication consultants, is founded in communication research respected since the 1940s. At that time, Paul Lazarsfeld, Bernard Berelson, and Hazel Gaudet wrote *The People's Choice*, in which they identified the crucial role of opinion leaders in changing behavior. Again, we've refused to listen.

Supervisor briefings are an effective way to gain the acceptance of supervisors. Supervisor briefings are face-to-face meetings between a senior manager working on the change and a small group of frontline supervisors. These briefings usually occur in two rounds. In the first round, the senior manager explains the change and supervisors make recommendations. (See the table "Ask Supervisors for Their Opinions.") After this round, the

---

Ask Supervisors for Their Opinions

The First Round of Supervisor Briefings: Collecting Recommendations

What to Do	Why
One senior manager meets with eight to ten supervisors.	Don't give the impression that you are afraid of your subordinates and need to travel in a gang.
Bring a single piece of paper (copies for everyone) divided into two parts: willing to change and not willing to change.	Don't play games with these people. If you have no intention of changing something, make that clear from the beginning.
Describe items in the not-willing-to-change column; request recommendations for items in the willing-to-change column.	You are not there to argue, defend, or evaluate. Your job is to hear supervisors' opinions and report them to the senior-management change team.
Never give away the power to decide. Make it clear that power remains with the senior-management change team.	You are there to get supervisors' opinions, not their permission.
Never allow the meeting to go longer than 90 minutes.	Supervisors will become restless. Get into it, do your business, and get out of it.

senior manager reports the recommendations to the senior-management change team, and the group tries to work as many of the recommendations as possible into the plan. Remember, the degree to which supervisors will support your change depends on how many of their recommendations are used. This is the right time for compromise.

In the second round of briefings, the senior manager reports on the status of the recommendations and explains the final plan. (See the table "Give Them the Facts, Just the Facts.") Allow about two weeks to pass after the second round of briefings, and then release sto-

---

Give Them the Facts, Just the Facts

The Second Round of Supervisor Briefings: Reporting Back

What to Do	Why
The same manager meets with the same supervisors.	Supervisors don't want to deal with an abstraction—management; they want to deal with a person.
Bring a single piece of paper (copies for everyone) listing the supervisors' recommendations. Next to each one, explain briefly why it was accepted or rejected. Answer questions but do not argue or excessively defend.	You are not trying to convince the supervisors; you are there to let them know what has happened to their recommendations.
Distribute a change booklet to each supervisor. Describe the major parts of the change as detailed in the change booklet.	You are preparing the supervisors for the face-to-face conversations they will have with their subordinates.

ries in the company's newspaper and in informational sheets.

Supervisor briefings may not sound revolutionary, but they are. In a company that institutes such briefings, a frontline employee who wants to know what's happening has only one way to get that information: by asking the supervisor. And that information probably will be communicated one-on-one and will be in the supervisor's own words. No big meeting, no grand announcement, no executive road shows, no speeches relayed by satellite. All the resources previously spent communicating indiscriminately are aimed at communicating with supervisors, who are given information, influence, and thereby increased power and status. As a result, they are more likely to help implement change.

Max was the kind of supervisor who could lead his team to fix a machine by listening to it over the phone.

Max, the Supervisor

Max is a supervisor in an integrated steel mill. The personnel department says that Max has the worst employees in the company. How do they know this? They give him the worst employees. Max's department also has the least downtime, the fewest discipline problems, the lowest rate of absenteeism, and the best safety record in the company.

Max's reputation is formidable. According to one account, maintenance workers were under tremendous pressure to repair a continuous-casting machine. Unfortunately, Max was away on vacation. At 2 a.m., the workers finally tracked him down in a tavern hundreds of miles away. Mechanics held the telephone to the ailing machine while Max listened for several minutes without speaking. Max then directed an hour's worth of instructions over the phone—and the machine ran perfectly.

Max's company is undergoing major change, technically and culturally. One afternoon, the mill is stopped. Four hundred frontline workers gather in the cafeteria. Under a banner that reads Steel: Our Future, senior managers announce new capital investments in pulverized-coal injection, experiments with thin-slab casting, and an electric-arc furnace. Senior managers then describe the cultural changes.

Max, sitting shoulder-to-shoulder with his crew, hears for the first time that the company will no longer have supervisors. Supervisors will become TFs (team facilitators). Max's maintenance department will become a CAT (committee action team). Every frontline employee will be empowered to submit QIOs (quality improvement opportunities). Max is told that he will be helped with the cultural transition: Professors from the university will run courses to help him "evolve" from a "boss" into a "facilitator of his CAT's QIOs."

Could this possibly be the best way to communicate these important changes to Max? Is it any wonder that he has doubts about the competence of the company's senior managers? But don't blame them; they're experts in steel. Blame their communication advisers. While the launch of Steel: Our Future is embarrassing, it is not a tragedy. The tragedy has yet to occur.

In the days following the presentation, frontline workers make their way to Max's shabby office. Sticking their heads in, they ask, "What do you think?" This is the moment that matters. What happened in the cafeteria is irrelevant. What happens in Max's office will determine how long it will take to make a return on this massive investment in new equipment. Following the presentation, the communication consultants pack their bags and go home. They think the communication is over. Little do they know that the real communication has not even begun.

So what will Max say? He has no inside information. He knows no more than any frontline employee. Max's opinions seem to carry absolutely no weight. Instead of treating him as someone important, management rounded him up with his subordinates and dumped a bucket of jargon on him. The only words specifically targeted to supervisors were a threat: "There will be no place in the company for supervisors who fail to make the transition to team facilitators." What is Max going to say about the change? He's going to say, "It's [expletive]." That is the tragedy.

The Steel: Our Future campaign ignores its major challenge: getting frontline support for the new technology. The front line has every reason to withhold its cooperation. In fact, the front line has 800 reasons: the number of jobs eliminated from Max's division as a result of previous capital investments. Workers believe that slowing down the implementation may postpone further job losses. Slowing it down months would be good; slowing it down years would be even better.

During the presentation, the CEO said that the technology was not intended to replace workers. But the workers need to hear that *Max* believes that the new technology is not intended to replace jobs. And that will happen only if managers convince Max and his fellow supervisors.

Let's not overstate the damage caused by poor communication. Max's company will end up implementing its changes. The front line will eventually see that job reductions are not the goal. And the organization will deliver better steel more quickly to its customers. The problem, however, is that the changes will take longer than they need to. In their article "Why Some Factories Are More Productive than Others" (*Harvard Business Review* September–October 1986), Robert H. Hayes and Kim B. Clark describe factories in which as much as two-thirds of the productivity gain from new equipment occurred as a result of employee learning. Employees experiment with and modify new equipment and con-necting equipment. Failure to gain acceptance for new technology, according to Hayes and Clark, can postpone return-on-investment goals by as much as a year. Max's crew will be eager to learn about the new technology if Max endorses it. And Max is more likely to do so if the company treats him as a vital source of information and as an opinion leader.

Our advice contradicts the widely publicized image of the charismatic executive rousing the troops through impassioned speeches, but it makes a lot of sense to workers on the front line of any organization. Senior managers must realize that employees will change the way they go about their jobs only if they learn about what is expected of them from a familiar and credible source. Communication between frontline supervisors and employees counts the most toward changed behav-ior where it matters the most: at the front line.

Notes

1. David T. Bastien, "Common Patterns of Behavior and Communication in Corporate Mergers and Acquisitions," *Human Resource Management*, spring 1987; Jeanette A.

Davy, Angelo Kinicki, Christine Scheck, and John Kilroy, "Acquisitions Make Employees Worry," *Personnel Administrator*, August 1989; David M. Schweiger and Angelo S. Denisi, "Communication with Employees Following a Merger: A Longitudinal Field Experiment," *Academy of Management Journal*, March 1991.

2. For Colgate-Palmolive, see Isadore Barmash, "More Substance than Show," *Across the Board*, May 1993; for Royal Bank of Scotland, see Mary Williams, "Fair Comment," *Personnel Today*, March 1993; for British Telecom, see "Natural Selection: BT's Programme of Voluntary Redundancy," *IRS Employment Trends*, April 1993; for Whirlpool, see Peter Moore, "Turning the Tide at Whirlpool," *Communication World*, March 1994; for Rank Xerox, see Heather Falconer, "Keeping Staff in the Know," *Personnel Today*, March 1992.

Originally published in May–June 1996
Reprint 96304

How Management Teams Can Have a Good Fight

KATHLEEN M. EISENHARDT,

JEAN L. KAHWAJY, AND

L.J. BOURGEOIS III

Executive Summary

TOP-LEVEL MANAGERS KNOW that conflict over issues is natural and even necessary. Management teams that challenge one another's thinking develop a more complete understanding of their choices, create a richer range of options, and make better decisions.

But the challenge—familiar to anyone who has ever been part of a management team—is to keep constructive conflict over issues from degenerating into interpersonal conflict.

From their research on the interplay of conflict, politics, and speed in the decision-making process of management teams, the authors have distilled a set of six tactics characteristic of high-performing teams:

- They work with more, rather than less, information.

- They develop multiple alternatives to enrich debate.

- They make an effort to inject humor into the workplace.

- They maintain a balanced corporate power structure.

- They resolve issues without forcing a consensus.

These tactics work because they keep conflict focused on issues; foster collaborative, rather than competitive, relations among team members; and create a sense of fairness in the decision-making process.

Without conflict, groups lose their effectiveness. Managers often become withdrawn and only superficially harmonious. The alternative to conflict is not usually agreement but rather apathy and disengagement, which open the doors to a primary cause of major corporate debacles: groupthink.

TOP MANAGERS ARE OFTEN STYMIED by the difficulties of managing conflict. They know that conflict over issues is natural and even necessary. Reasonable people, making decisions under conditions of uncertainty, are likely to have honest disagreements over the best path for their company's future. Management teams whose members challenge one another's thinking develop a more complete understanding of the choices, create a richer range of options, and ultimately make the kinds of

The challenge is to encourage members of management teams to argue without destroying their ability to work together.

effective decisions necessary in today's competitive environments.

But, unfortunately, healthy conflict can quickly turn unproductive. A comment meant as a substantive remark can be interpreted as a personal attack. Anxiety and frustration over difficult choices can evolve into anger directed at colleagues. Personalities frequently become intertwined with issues. Because most executives pride themselves on being rational decision makers, they find it difficult even to acknowledge—let alone manage—this emotional, irrational dimension of their behavior.

The challenge—familiar to anyone who has ever been part of a management team—is to keep constructive conflict over issues from degenerating into dysfunctional interpersonal conflict, to encourage managers to argue without destroying their ability to work as a team. (See the exhibit "How Teams Argue but Still Get Along.")

How Teams Argue but Still Get Along

Tactic ⟶	Strategy
Base discussion on current, factual information. Develop multiple alternatives to enrich the debate.	Focus on issues, not personalities.
Rally around goals. Inject humor into the decision-making process.	Frame decisions as collaborations aimed at achieving the best possible solution for the company.
Maintain a balanced power structure. Resolve issues without forcing consensus.	Establish a sense of fairness and equity in the process.

We have been researching the interplay of conflict, politics, and speed in strategic decision making by top-management teams for the past ten years. In one study, we had the opportunity to observe closely the work of a dozen top-management teams in technology-based companies. All the companies competed in fast changing, competitive global markets. Thus all the teams had to make high-stakes decisions in the face of considerable uncertainty and under pressure to move quickly. Each team consisted of between five and nine executives; we were allowed to question them individually and also to observe their interactions firsthand as we tracked specific strategic decisions in the making. The study's design gives us a window on conflict as top-management teams actually experience it and highlights the role of emotion in business decision making.

In 4 of the 12 companies, there was little or no substantive disagreement over major issues and therefore little conflict to observe. But the other 8 companies experienced considerable conflict. In 4 of them, the top-management teams handled conflict in a way that avoided interpersonal hostility or discord. We've called those companies Bravo Microsystems, Premier Technologies, Star Electronics, and Triumph Computers. Executives in those companies referred to their colleagues as "smart," "team player," and "best in the business." They described the way they work as a team as "open," "fun," and "productive." The executives vigorously debated the issues, but they wasted little time on politicking and posturing. As one put it, "I really don't have time." Another said, "We don't gloss over the issues; we hit them straight on. But we're not political."

Still another observed of her company's management team, "We scream a lot, then laugh, and then resolve the issue."

The other four companies in which issues were contested were less successful at avoiding interpersonal conflict. We've called those companies Andromeda Processing, Mega Software, Mercury Microdevices, and Solo Systems. Their top teams were plagued by intense animosity. Executives often failed to cooperate, rarely talking with one another, tending to fragment into cliques, and openly displaying their frustration and anger. When executives described their colleagues to us, they used words such as "manipulative," "secretive," "burned out," and "political."

The teams with minimal interpersonal conflict were able to separate substantive issues from those based on personalities. They managed to disagree over questions of strategic significance and still get along with one another. How did they do that? After analyzing our observations of the teams' behavior, we found that their companies used the same six tactics for managing interpersonal conflict. Team members

- worked with more, rather than less, information and debated on the basis of facts;

- developed multiple alternatives to enrich the level of debate;

- shared commonly agreed-upon goals;

- injected humor into the decision process;

- maintained a balanced power structure;

- resolved issues without forcing consensus.

Those tactics were usually more implicit than explicit in the decision-making work of the management teams, and if the tactics were given names, the names varied from one organization to the next. Nonetheless, the consistency with which all four companies employed all six tactics is testimony to their effectiveness. Perhaps most surprising was the fact that the tactics did not delay—and often accelerated—the pace at which the teams were able to make decisions.

Focus on the Facts

Some managers believe that working with too much data will increase interpersonal conflict by expanding the range of issues for debate. We found that more information is better—if the data are objective and up-to-date—because it encourages people to focus on issues, not personalities. At Star Electronics, for example, the members of the top-management team typically examined a wide variety of operating measures on a monthly, weekly, and even daily basis. They claimed to "measure everything." In particular, every week they fixed their attention on indicators such as bookings, backlogs, margins, engineering milestones, cash, scrap, and work-in-process. Every month, they reviewed an even more comprehensive set of measures that gave them extensive knowledge of what was actually happening in the corporation. As one executive noted, "We have very strong controls."

Star's team also relied on facts about the external environment. One senior executive was charged with tracking such moves by competitors as product introductions, price changes, and ad campaigns. A second followed the latest technical developments through his network of contacts in universities and other companies. "We over-M.B.A. it," said the CEO, characterizing Star's zealous pursuit of data. Armed with the facts, Star's executives had an extraordinary grasp of the details of their business, allowing them to focus debate on critical issues and avoid useless arguments rooted in ignorance.

At Triumph Computer, we found a similar dedication to current facts. The first person the new CEO hired was an individual to track the progress of engineering-development projects, the new-product lifeblood of the company. Such knowledge allowed the top-management team to work from a common base of facts.

In the absence of good data, executives waste time in pointless debate over opinions. Some resort to self-aggrandizement and ill-formed guesses about how the world might be. People—and not issues—become the focus of disagreement. The result is interpersonal conflict. In such companies, top managers are often poorly informed both about internal operations, such as bookings and engineering milestones, and about external issues, such as competing products. They collect data narrowly and infrequently. In these companies, the vice presidents of finance, who oversee internal data collection, are usually weak. They were often described by people in the companies we studied as "inexperienced" or "detached." In contrast, the vice president of finance at Premier Technologies, a company with little interpersonal conflict, was described as being central to taking "the constant pulse of how the firm is doing."

More information is better. There is a direct link between reliance on facts and low levels of interpersonal conflict.

Management teams troubled by interpersonal conflict rely more on hunches and guesses than on current data. When they consider facts, they are more likely to examine a past measure, such as profitability, which is both historical and highly refined. These teams favor planning based on extrapolation and intuitive attempts to predict the future, neither of which yields current or factual results. Their conversations are more subjective. The CEO of one of the four high-conflict teams told us his interest in operating numbers was "minimal," and he described his goals as "subjective." At another such company, senior managers saw the CEO as "visionary" and "a little detached from the day-to-day operations." Compare those executives with the CEO of Bravo Microsystems, who had a reputation for being a "pragmatic numbers guy."

There is a direct link between reliance on facts and low levels of interpersonal conflict. Facts let people move quickly to the central issues surrounding a strategic choice. Decision makers don't become bogged down in arguments over what the facts *might* be. More important, reliance on current data grounds strategic discussions in reality. Facts (such as current sales, market share, R&D expenses, competitors' behavior, and manufacturing yields) depersonalize the discussion because they are not someone's fantasies, guesses, or self-serving desires. In the absence of facts, individuals' motives are likely to become suspect. Building decisions on facts creates a culture that emphasizes issues instead of personalities.

Multiply the Alternatives

Some managers believe that they can reduce conflict by focusing on only one or two alternatives, thus minimizing the dimensions over which people can disagree. But, in fact, teams with low incidences of interpersonal conflict do just the opposite. They deliberately develop multiple alternatives, often considering four or five options at once. To promote debate, managers will even introduce options they do not support.

For example, Triumph's new CEO was determined to improve the company's lackluster performance. When he arrived, new products were stuck in development, and investors were getting anxious. He launched a fact-gathering exercise and asked senior executives to develop alternatives. In less than two months, they developed four. The first was to sell some of the company's technology. The second was to undertake a major strategic redirection, using the base technology to enter a new market. The third was to redeploy engineering resources and adjust the marketing approach. The final option was to sell the company.

Working together to shape those options enhanced the group's sense of teamwork while promoting a more creative view of Triumph's competitive situation and its technical competencies. As a result, the team ended up combining elements of several options in a way that was more robust than any of the options were individually.

The other teams we observed with low levels of interpersonal conflict also tended to develop multiple options to make major decisions. Star, for example, faced a cash flow crisis caused by explosive growth. Its executives considered, among other choices, arranging for lines of credit from banks, selling additional stock, and forming strategic alliances with several partners. At Bravo, managers explicitly relied on three kinds of alternatives: sincere proposals that the proponent actually backed; support for someone else's proposal, even if only for the sake of argument; and insincere alternatives proposed just to expand the number of options.

There are several reasons why considering multiple alternatives may lower interpersonal conflict. For one, it diffuses conflict: choices become less black and white, and individuals gain more room to vary the degree of their support over a range of choices. Managers can more easily shift positions without losing face.

Generating options is also a way to bring managers together in a common and inherently stimulating task. It concentrates their energy on solving problems, and it increases the likelihood of obtaining integrative solutions—alternatives that incorporate the views of a greater number of the decision makers. In generating multiple alternatives, managers do not stop at obvious solutions; rather, they continue generating further—usually more original—options. The process in itself is creative and fun, setting a positive tone for substantive, instead of interpersonal, conflict.

In teams that vigorously debate just one or two options, conflict often turns personal, as positions harden.

By contrast, in teams that vigorously debate just one or two options, conflict often does turn personal. At Solo Systems, for instance, the top-management team considered entering a new business area as a way to boost the company's performance. They debated this alternative versus the status quo but failed to consider other options. Individual executives became increasingly entrenched on one side of the debate or the other. As positions hardened, the conflict became more pointed and personal. The animosity grew so great that a major proponent of change quit the company in disgust while the rest of the team either disengaged or slipped into intense and dysfunctional politicking.

Create Common Goals

A third tactic for minimizing destructive conflict involves framing strategic choices as collaborative, rather than competitive, exercises. Elements of collaboration and competition coexist within any management team: executives share a stake in the company's performance, yet their personal ambitions may make them rivals for power. The successful groups we studied consistently framed their decisions as collaborations in which it was in everyone's interest to achieve the best possible solution for the collective.

They did so by creating a common goal around which the team could rally. Such goals do not imply homogeneous thinking, but they do require everyone to share a vision. As Steve Jobs, who is associated with three high-profile Silicon Valley companies—Apple, NeXT, and Pixar—has advised, "It's okay to spend a lot of time arguing about which route to take to San Francisco when everyone wants to end up there, but a lot of time gets wasted in such arguments if one person wants to go to San Francisco and another secretly wants to go to San Diego."

Teams hobbled by conflict lack common goals. Team members perceive themselves to be in competition with one another and, surprisingly, tend to frame decisions negatively, as reactions to threats. At Andromeda Processing, for instance, the team focused on responding to a particular instance of poor performance, and team members tried to pin the blame on one another. That negative framing contrasts with the positive approach taken by Star Electronics executives, who, sharing a common goal, viewed a cash crisis not as a threat but as an opportunity to "build the biggest war chest" for an impending competitive battle. At a broad level, Star's executives shared the goal of creating "*the* computer firm of the decade." As one Star executive told us, "We take a corporate, not a functional, viewpoint most of the time."

Likewise, all the management team members we interviewed at Premier Technologies agreed that their common goal—their rallying cry—was to build "the best damn machine on the market." Thus in their debates they could disagree about critical technical alternatives—in-house versus offshore manufacturing options, for example, or alternative distribution channels—without letting the conflict turn personal.

Many studies of group decision making and intergroup conflict demonstrate that common goals build team cohesion by stressing the shared interest of all team members in the outcome of the debate. When team members are working toward a common goal, they are less likely to see themselves as individual winners and losers and are far more likely to perceive the opinions of others correctly and to learn from them. We observed that when executives lacked common goals, they tended to be closed-minded and more likely to misinterpret and blame one another.

Use Humor

Teams that handle conflict well make explicit—and often even contrived—attempts to relieve tension and at the same time promote a collaborative esprit by making their business fun. They emphasize the excitement of fast-paced competition, not the stress of competing in brutally tough and uncertain markets.

All the teams with low interpersonal conflict described ways in which they used humor on the job. Executives at Bravo Microsystems enjoyed playing gags around the office. For example, pink plastic flamingos— souvenirs from a customer—graced Bravo's otherwise impeccably decorated headquarters. Similarly, Triumph Computers' top managers held a monthly "dessert pig-out," followed by group weight watching. Those seemingly trivial activities were part of the CEO's deliberate plan to make work more fun, despite the pressures of the industry. At Star Electronics, making the company "a fun place" was an explicit goal for the top-management team. Laughter was common during management meetings. Practical jokes were popular at Star, where executives—along with other employees—always celebrated Halloween and April Fools' Day.

At each of these companies, executives acknowledged that at least some of the attempts at humor were contrived—even forced. Even so, they helped to release tension and promote collaboration.

Humor was strikingly absent in the teams marked by high interpersonal conflict. Although pairs of individuals were sometimes friends, team members shared no group social activities beyond a standard holiday party or two, and there were no conscious attempts to create humor. Indeed, the climate in which decisions were made was often just the opposite—hostile and stressful.

Humor works as a defense mechanism to protect people from the stressful and threatening situations that commonly arise in the course of making strategic decisions. It helps people distance themselves psychologically by putting those situations into a broader life context, often through the use of irony. Humor—with its ambiguity—can also blunt the threatening edge of negative information. Speakers can say in jest things that might otherwise give offense because the message is simultaneously serious and not serious. The recipient is allowed to save face by receiving the serious message while appearing not to do so. The result is communication of difficult information in a more tactful and less personally threatening way.

Humor can also move decision making into a collaborative rather than competitive frame through its powerful effect on mood. According to a large body of research, people in a positive mood tend to be not only more optimistic but also more forgiving of others and creative in seeking solutions. A positive mood triggers a more accurate perception of others' arguments because people in a good mood tend to relax their defensive barriers and so can listen more effectively.

Balance the Power Structure

We found that managers who believe that their team's decision-making process is fair are more likely to accept decisions without resentment, even when they do not agree with them. But when they believe the process is unfair, ill will easily grows into interpersonal conflict. A fifth tactic for taming interpersonal conflict, then, is to create a sense of fairness by balancing power within the management team.

Our research suggests that autocratic leaders who manage through highly centralized power structures often generate high levels of interpersonal friction. At the other extreme, weak leaders also engender interpersonal conflict because the power vacuum at the top encourages managers to jockey for position. Interpersonal conflict is lowest in what we call *balanced power structures*, those in which the CEO is more powerful than the other members of the top-management team, but the members do wield substantial power, especially in their

Autocratic leaders often tend to generate high levels of interpersonal friction.

own well-defined areas of responsibility. In balanced power structures, all executives participate in strategic decisions.

At Premier Technologies, for example, the CEO—described by others as a "team player"—was definitely the most powerful figure. But each executive was the most powerful decision maker in some clearly defined area. In addition, the entire team participated in all significant decisions. The CEO, one executive observed, "depends on picking good people and letting them operate."

The CEO of Bravo Microsystems, another company with a balanced power structure, summarized his philosophy as "making quick decisions involving as many people as possible." We watched the Bravo team over several months as it grappled with a major strategic redirection. After many group discussions, the final decision was made at a multiday retreat involving the whole team.

In contrast, the leaders of the teams marked by extensive interpersonal conflict were either highly autocratic or weak. The CEO at Mercury Microdevices, for example, was the principal decision maker. There was a substantial gap in power between him and the rest of the team. In the decision we tracked, the CEO dominated the process from start to finish, identifying the problem, defining the analysis, and making the choice. Team members described the CEO as "strong" and "dogmatic." As one of them put it, "When Bruce makes a decision, it's like God!"

At Andromeda, the CEO exercised only modest power, and areas of responsibility were blurred within the top-management team, where power was diffuse and ambiguous. Senior executives had to politick amongst themselves to get anything accomplished, and they reported intense frustration with the confusion that existed at the top.

Most executives expected to control some significant aspect of their business but not the entirety. When they lacked power—because of either an autocrat or a power vacuum—they became frustrated by their inability to make significant decisions. Instead of team members, they became politicians. As one executive explained, "We're all jockeying for our spot in the pecking order." Another described "maneuvering for the CEO's ear."

The situations we observed are consistent with classic social-psychology studies of leadership. For example, in a study from the 1960s, Ralph White and Ronald Lippitt examined the effects of different leadership styles on boys in social clubs. They found that boys with democratic leaders—the situation closest to our balanced power structure—showed spontaneous interest in their activities. The boys were highly satisfied, and within their groups there were many friendly remarks, much praise, and significant collaboration. Under weak leaders, the boys were disorganized, inefficient, and dissatisfied. But the worst case was autocratic rule, under which the boys were hostile and aggressive, occasionally directing physical violence against innocent scapegoats. In imbalanced power situations, we observed adult displays of verbal aggression that colleagues described as violent. One executive talked about being "caught in the cross fire." Another described a colleague as "a gun about to go off." A third spoke about "being beat up" by the CEO.

Seek Consensus with Qualification

Balancing power is one tactic for building a sense of fairness. Finding an appropriate way to resolve conflict over issues is another—and, perhaps, the more crucial. In our research, the teams that managed conflict effectively all used the same approach to resolving substantive conflict. It is a two-step process that some executives call *consensus with qualification*. It works like this: executives talk over an issue and try to reach consensus. If they can, the decision is made. If they can't, the most relevant senior manager makes the decision, guided by input from the rest of the group.

When a competitor launched a new product attacking Premier Technologies in its biggest market, for example, there was sharp disagreement about how to respond. Some executives wanted to shift R&D resources to counter this competitive move, even at the risk of diverting engineering talent from a more innovative product then in design. Others argued that Premier should simply repackage an existing product, adding a few novel features. A third group felt that the threat was not serious enough to warrant a major response.

Executives may believe that consensus is always possible, but insisting on agreement can lead to endless haggling.

After a series of meetings over several weeks, the group failed to reach consensus. So the CEO and his marketing vice president made the decision. As the CEO explained, "The functional heads do the talking. I pull the trigger." Premier's executives were comfortable with this arrangement—even those who did not agree with the outcome—because everyone had had a voice in the process.

People usually associate consensus with harmony, but we found the opposite: teams that insisted on resolving substantive conflict by forcing consensus tended to display the most interpersonal conflict. Executives sometimes have the unrealistic view that consensus is always possible, but such a naïve insistence on consensus can lead to endless haggling. As the vice president of engineering at Mega Software put it, "Consensus means that everyone has veto power. Our products were too late, and they were too expensive." At Andromeda, the CEO wanted his executives to reach consensus, but persistent differences of opinion remained. The debate dragged on for months, and the frustration mounted until some top managers simply gave up. They just wanted a decision, any decision. One was finally made when several executives who favored one point of view left the company. The price of consensus was a decimated team.

In a team that insists on consensus, deadlines can cause executives to sacrifice fairness and thus weaken the team's support for the final decision. At Andromeda, executives spent months analyzing their industry and developing a shared perspective on important trends for the future, but they could never focus on making the decision. The decision-making process dragged on. Finally, as the deadline of a board meeting drew imminent, the CEO formulated and announced a choice—one that had never even been mentioned in the earlier discussions. Not surprisingly, his team was angry and upset. Had he been less insistent on reaching a consensus, the CEO would not have felt forced by the deadline to act so arbitrarily. (See "Building a Fighting Team" at the end of this article.)

How does consensus with qualification create a sense of fairness? A body of research on procedural justice shows that process fairness, which involves significant participation and influence by all concerned, is enormously important to most people. Individuals are willing to accept outcomes they dislike if they believe that the process by which those results came about was fair. Most people want their opinions to be considered seriously but are willing to accept that those opinions cannot always prevail. That is precisely what occurs in consensus with qualification. As one executive at Star said, "I'm happy just to bring up my opinions."

Apart from fairness, there are several other reasons why consensus with qualification is an important deterrent to interpersonal conflict. It assumes that conflict is natural and not a sign of interpersonal dysfunction. It gives managers added influence when the decision affects their part of the organization in particular, thus balancing managers' desires to be heard with the need to make a choice. It is an equitable and egalitarian process of decision making that encourages everyone to bring ideas to the table but clearly delineates how the decision will be made.

Finally, consensus with qualification is fast. Processes that require consensus tend to drag on endlessly, frustrating managers with what they see as time-consuming and useless debate. It's not surprising that the managers end up blaming their frustration on the shortcomings of their colleagues and not on the poor conflict-resolution process.

Linking Conflict, Speed, and Performance

A considerable body of academic research has demonstrated that conflict over issues is not only likely within top-management teams but also valuable. Such conflict provides executives with a more inclusive range of information, a deeper understanding of the issues, and a richer set of possible solutions. That was certainly the case in the companies we studied. The evidence also overwhelmingly indicates that where there is little conflict over issues, there is also likely to be poor decision making. "Groupthink" has been a primary cause of major corporate- and public-policy debacles. And although it may seem counterintuitive, we found that the teams that engaged in healthy conflict over issues not only made better decisions but moved more quickly as well.

Without conflict, groups lose their effectiveness. Managers often become withdrawn and only superficially harmonious. Indeed, we found that the alternative to conflict is usually not agreement but apathy and disengagement. Teams unable to foster substantive conflict ultimately achieve, on average, lower performance. Among the companies that we observed, low-conflict teams tended to forget to consider key issues or were simply unaware of important aspects of their strategic situation. They missed opportunities to question falsely limiting assumptions or to generate significantly different alternatives. Not surprisingly, their actions were often easy for competitors to anticipate.

In fast-paced markets, successful strategic decisions are most likely to be made by teams that promote active and broad conflict over issues without sacrificing speed. The key to doing so is to mitigate interpersonal conflict.

Building a Fighting Team

HOW CAN MANAGERS encourage the kind of substantive debate over issues that leads to better decision making? We found five approaches that help generate constructive disagreement within a team:

1. **Assemble a heterogeneous team, including diverse ages, genders, functional backgrounds, and industry experience.** If everyone in the executive meetings looks alike and sounds alike, then the chances are excellent that they probably think alike, too.

2. **Meet together as a team regularly and often.** Team members that don't know one another well don't know one another's positions on issues, impairing their ability to argue effectively. Frequent interaction builds the mutual confidence and familiarity team members require to express dissent.

3. **Encourage team members to assume roles beyond their obvious product, geographic, or functional responsibilities.** Devil's advocates, sky-gazing visionaries, and action-oriented executives can work together to ensure that all sides of an issue are considered.

4. **Apply multiple mind-sets to any issue.** Try role-playing, putting yourself in your competitors' shoes, or conducting war games. Such techniques create fresh perspectives

and engage team members, spurring interest in problem solving.

5. **Actively manage conflict.** Don't let the team acquiesce too soon or too easily. Identify and treat apathy early, and don't confuse a lack of conflict with agreement. Often, what passes for consensus is really disengagement.

Originally published in July–August 1997
Reprint 97402

About the Contributors

CHRIS ARGYRIS is the James Conant Professor of Education and Organizational Behavior Emeritus at Harvard University. He has consulted to numerous private and governmental organizations. He has received many awards including eleven honorary degrees and Life Time Contribution Awards from the Academy of Management, American Psychological Association, and American Society of Training Directors. His most recent books are *On Organizational Learning* and *The Next Challenge: In Leadership, Learning, Change, and Commitment.*

FERNANDO BARTOLOMÉ is currently Professor of Management at the Instituto de Empresa in Madrid, Spain, and Visiting Professor of Organizational Behaviour at INSEAD. He also works as a management development consultant to multinational companies in the United States, Europe, Latin America, and Asia. His main areas of interest are individual and interpersonal behavior. Among his publications are "Executives as Human Beings," "The Work Alibi," and "The Manager: Master and Servant of Power," published by the *Harvard Business Review.* His book *Must Success Cost So Much?,* coauthored with Paul A. Lee Evans, describes their research on the effects of professional life on the private lives of executives.

L.J. BOURGEOIS III is a professor of business administration at the Darden Graduate School of Business. He has consulted for a variety of North and Latin American, European,

Asian, and Australian corporations on strategic management, corporate mission, and top-management team building, and has designed and conducted various seminars in strategic thinking. He is the author of *Strategic Management: From Concept to Implementation,* as well as articles in various management journals.

KATHLEEN M. EISENHARDT is a professor of strategy and organization in the School of Engineering, Stanford University, and coauthor of *Competing on the Edge: Strategy as Structured Chaos* (HBS Press, 1998). Her research and teaching focus on managing in high-velocity, intensely competitive markets. Eisenhardt's awards include the Pacific Telesis Foundation for her ideas on fast strategic decision making, the Stern Award for work on strategic alliances in entrepreneurial firms, and the Whittemore Prize for her writing on organizing global firms in rapidly changing markets.

At the time his article appeared in the *Harvard Business Review,* ANTONY JAY was chairman of Video Arts, Ltd., a British film production and distribution company. Formerly, he was a BBC television producer and executive. He is the author of *Management and Machiavelli* and *Corporation Man,* and was responsible, with John Cleese of *Monty Python,* for a series of comedy training films for industry and management.

JEAN L. KAHWAJY coaches senior executives and teams, offering more effective approaches to meeting the challenges of change, communication, and negotiation. For ten years she has been a management consultant in strategy development and decision quality, and she regularly gives seminars worldwide on these topics. The author of several articles on organizational design, mitigating interpersonal conflict, and top management team decision making, Ms. Kahwajy is currently completing her doctoral studies at Stanford University investigating the social and psychological forces that influence decision makers—in particular the role of receiving others.

T.J. LARKIN and **SANDAR LARKIN** are partners with Larkin Communication Consulting. Their consulting firm helps large companies communicate major change to employees. The Larkins have also written *Communicating Change,* a McGraw-Hill bookstore best-seller. Larkin Communication Consulting has offices in New York City, London, and Melbourne, Australia.

MICHAEL B. MCCASKEY was associate professor of organizational behavior at the Harvard Business School when his article was first published. At the time, he studied how managers cope with ill-defined situations, citing nonverbal communication and imagery as useful tools for dealing with ambiguity. He served as president and chief executive officer of the Chicago Bears and was named the Executive of the Year by *Sporting News* in 1985.

At the time his article appeared in the *Harvard Business Review,* **RALPH G. NICHOLS** was the head of a communications program at the University of Minnesota. Prior to that, he was president of the National Society for the Study of Communication. He also served on the editorial boards of two national publications and was president of the State Speech Teachers Associations in Minnesota and Iowa.

When his article appeared in the *Harvard Business Review,* **GEORGE M. PRINCE** was chairman of Synectics, Inc., a Cambridge, Massachusetts, consulting firm specializing in improving the creativity and problem-solving ability of client management.

At the time his article appeared in the *Harvard Business Review,* **LEONARD A. STEVENS** was a freelance writer and consultant on oral presentation to a number of leading companies and was affiliated with Management Development Associates of New York. He collaborated with Ralph G. Nichols on several articles.

Index